ROMANTIC QUILTS

Lush and Lovely Projects for Your Home

from *Australian Patchwork & Quilting Magazine*

Martingale®
& COMPANY

Romantic Quilts:
Lush and Lovely Projects for Your Home
© 2004 by Martingale & Company®

That Patchwork Place® is an imprint of
Martingale & Company®.

Martingale & Company
20205 144th Avenue NE
Woodinville, WA 98072-8478
www.martingale-pub.com

Printed in China

09 08 07 06 05 04   8 7 6 5 4 3 2 1

**Library of Congress Cataloging-in-Publication
Data**

Romantic quilts: lush and lovely projects for your
home from Australian patchwork & quilting
magazine / [edited by Laurie Bevan].
    p. cm.
The quilt designs in this book were originally
published by Express Publications Pty., Ltd.
Photographs courtesy of Express Publications.
   ISBN 1-56477-536-4
  1. Patchwork—Patterns. 2. Quilting—Patterns.
  3. Patchwork quilts.
I. Bevan, Laurie.
   TT835.R659 2004
   746.46'041—dc22
                             2003021773

Credits

President ✒ Nancy J. Martin

CEO ✒ Daniel J. Martin

Publisher ✒ Jane Hamada

Editorial Director ✒ Mary V. Green

Managing Editor ✒ Tina Cook

Technical Editor ✒ Laurie Bevan

Copy Editor ✒ Liz McGehee

Design Director ✒ Stan Green

Illustrator ✒ Laurel Strand

Cover and Text Designer ✒ Shelly Garrison

Mission Statement

Dedicated to providing quality products and
service to inspire creativity.

CONTENTS

Introduction 🌷 5

Windy Hill Rose 🌷 7

Anna's Quilt 🌷 13

Springtime Daisies 🌷 17

Starry, Starry Night 🌷 23

Pretty Strippy 🌷 29

Hearts and Roses 🌷 35

Midsummer Blooms 🌷 49

Antique Puss in the Corner 🌷 57

Rose Dream 🌷 63

Blue Star Garden 🌷 69

Hearts and Bows 🌷 75

Spring Garden 🌷 81

Old-World Charm 🌷 93

Quiltmaking Basics 🌷 98

INTRODUCTION

A romantic quilt dresses up a room with elegance, and these beautiful quilts from creative Australian quiltmakers do just that. Made with lovely florals, pretty pastels, and vintage-style prints, they inspire us to relax—perhaps to enjoy a cup of tea, a good book, or a pleasant conversation.

Any of these projects, covered with hearts and flowers, would be perfect for a wedding gift. What lucky couple wouldn't feel special snuggled under a gorgeous quilt made with love?

At sweet sixteen, a young lady is looking for a little sophistication in her surroundings. This is a wonderful time to make her a new quilt. "Anna's Quilt" (page 13) was made for the quiltmaker's daughter—perhaps you know someone special who would enjoy it as well.

Do you have a large collection of floral fabrics? Try the paper-pieced "Starry, Starry Night" (page 23) or "Spring Garden" (page 81), which features quick-and-easy, folded-corner Flying Geese. Maybe you prefer pink and green pastels. In that case, "Springtime Daisies" (page 17), with blanket-stitch appliqué, or the traditionally pieced "Old-World Charm" (page 93) may be the quilts to inspire you. If a more old-fashioned look is your preference, then your first project should be "Hearts and Roses" (page 35) with its beautiful, floral appliqué border. Or try "Antique Puss in the Corner" (page 57), a traditional quilt from the 19th century.

Whichever projects you choose to make, I'm sure you'll be pleased with the easy-to-follow instructions, helpful illustrations, and wonderful photography. Whether you live Down Under or in Downtown, USA, these quilts are sure to add a touch of elegance to your home.

Laurie Bevan

Editor

Finished Quilt Size: 68½" x 68½" (173 cm square) ▼ Finished Block Size: 10" x 10" (25 cm x 25 cm)

WINDY HILL ROSE

"Windy Hill Rose" is a tribute to flowers, with a leafy outlook and vintage feel. Robyn Falloon's combination of six appliqué flowers and three Butterfly at the Cross blocks, pieced in rich burgundy and natural tones, lends this quilt a charming earthiness. Robyn sketched the flowers until she was happy with the results, ending with large floral appliqué pieces and an easy-to-manage border arrangement.

Materials

Amounts are based on 42"-wide (107 cm) fabric.

▼ 2¼ yards (1.9 m) of cream print for outer border

▼ 2¼ yards (2 m) of large-scale floral for pieced blocks, large setting triangles, and binding

▼ 1⅝ yards (1.5 m) of dark crimson print for inner borders

▼ ¾ yard (70 cm) of light print for pieced blocks and appliqué block background

▼ ¼ yard (20 cm) of dark burgundy print for pieced blocks

▼ ⅛ yard (10 cm) of light burgundy print for center of pieced blocks

▼ Assorted scrap fabrics of red, coral, gold, blue, and purple for appliqué flowers and buds

▼ Assorted scrap fabrics of green for appliqué stems and leaves

▼ 4⅜ yards (4 m) of backing fabric

▼ 74" x 74" (2 m x 2 m) piece of batting

Cutting

All cutting dimensions include ¼" seam allowances. Instructions are for cutting strips across the fabric width except where noted.

From the light print, cut:

▼ 6 squares, 11" x 11"

▼ 1 strip, 2⅞" wide; crosscut into 12 squares, 2⅞" x 2⅞"

From the dark burgundy print, cut:

▼ 1 strip, 2½" wide; crosscut into 12 squares, 2½" x 2½"

▼ 1 strip, 2⅞" wide; crosscut into 12 squares, 2⅞" x 2⅞"

From the large-scale floral, cut:

▼ 2 squares, 25" x 25"; cut squares once diagonally to yield 4 large setting triangles

▼ 1 strip, 2½" wide; crosscut into 12 squares, 2½" x 2½"

▼ 1 strip, 4½" wide; crosscut into 12 rectangles, 2½" x 4½"

▼ 8 binding strips, 2½" wide

From the light burgundy print, cut:

▼ 3 squares, 2½" x 2½"

From the dark crimson print, cut *lengthwise*:

▼ 4 strips, 2½" x 36"

▼ 4 strips, 2½" x 55"

From the cream print, cut *lengthwise*:

▼ 4 strips, 8½" x 76"

Butterfly at the Cross Blocks

1. Draw a diagonal line on the wrong side of the 12 light 2⅞" squares. Pair each square with a dark burgundy 2⅞" square, right sides together, and sew ¼" from each side of the line. Cut on the line and press the seam allowance of each square toward the dark burgundy.

Make 24.

2. Make four-patch units using the 2½" floral squares, the 2½" dark burgundy squares, and the triangle squares from step 1 as shown.

Make 12.

3. Make three blocks using the 12 floral rectangles, the three light burgundy squares, and the four-patch units from step 2 as shown.

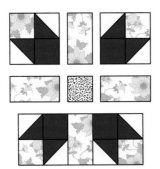

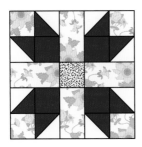

Make 3.

Appliqué Blocks

1. Fold each of the six 11" light print squares in half, then in quarters, and then in eighths on the diagonal, and press the folds lightly to create guidelines for the correct placement of the appliqué.

2. Use a photocopy machine to enlarge the block appliqué patterns on page 11. Trace the design onto each background square.

3. Using the appliqué method of your choice, trace and cut all the appliqué pieces. The flower and bud on each of the six blocks is a different color, and Robyn used a variety of green fabrics for the stems and leaves to create a realistic effect.

4. Appliqué the pieces of each section in numerical order, using thread to match each piece.

5. Embellish the appliqué on each block with embroidery, using a stem or outline stitch, straight stitch, French knots, and any other preferred embroidery stitches. The lines, dots, and other marks on the appliqué diagram represent placement of the embroidery embellishments. Robyn likes to use the beautiful variegated and overdyed silk threads available to create glistening veins on her appliqué leaves. Use one strand of thread and simple stem or outline stitches to embellish your work.

6. When the blocks are complete, press them gently from the wrong side first and then very lightly on the right side. Trim the blocks to 10½" square, making sure the design is centered on each block.

Quilt Assembly

1. Refer to the assembly diagram and arrange the six appliquéd blocks with the three pieced blocks into three rows of three blocks. Stitch the blocks together into rows and then press the seams in the first and third rows in the opposite direction to those in the second row.

2. Join the rows, butting the seams at the intersections, to form the center of the quilt top and press. The quilt top should measure 30½" square.

Assembly Diagram

Borders

1. The first inner dark crimson border has mitered corners. Add the 36"-long strips to the quilt center according to "Borders with Mitered Corners" on page 106.

2. Mark the middle of each side of the quilt top and each of the large floral setting triangles. Sew two triangles to the opposite sides of the quilt top, matching the marks, and press the seams toward the triangles. Join two more triangles to the remaining sides in the same manner.

3. The second inner dark crimson border has mitered corners like the first. Add the 55"-long strips to the quilt center as in step 1.

   Note: The second inner dark crimson border and the outer cream print border can be sewn to the quilt as a unit. Refer to the note in "Borders with Mitered Corners" on page 106.

4. The outer cream print border has mitered corners as well. Add the 76"-long strips to the quilt center as in step 1. The appliqué design for the two corners of the border is on page 11. Enlarge the design on a photocopy machine and trace it lightly onto the border.

Following the instructions for the appliqué blocks, cut out the flowers, centers, stems, and leaves and appliqué them in place.

Finishing

1. Cut the backing fabric into two equal lengths and remove the selvages. Sew the two pieces together along the length to make a backing with a horizontal seam; press the seam to one side.

2. Layer the backing, batting, and quilt top, smoothing each layer from the center outward as you go. Baste the three layers together using your preferred method.

3. Hand or machine quilt as desired. Robyn's quilt was machine quilted with meander quilting and a freehand floral design on the two dark crimson borders.

4. Remove the basting and trim the excess batting and backing fabric even with the edges of the quilt top. Join the eight 2½"-wide binding strips end to end using angled seams; press the seams open. Attach the binding to the quilt, referring to "Finishing" on page 109 for more details.

5. Label your quilt, including your name, the date, and any other relevant information.

Appliqué Patterns and Placement Diagrams

Add ¼" seam allowance for hand appliqué.

Corner Appliqué Patterns
Enlarge 250%.

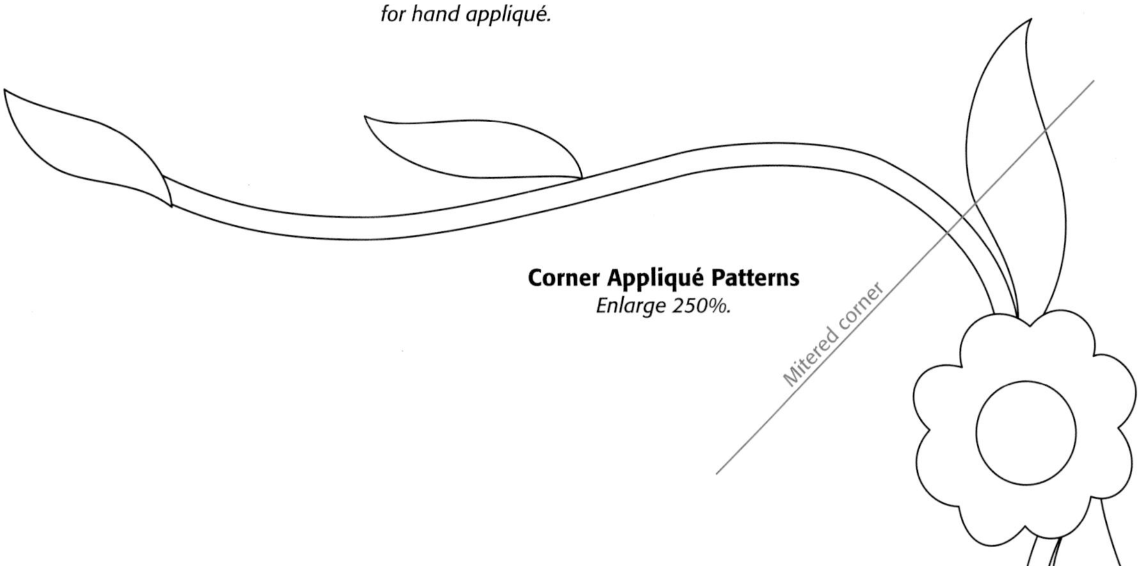

Mitered corner

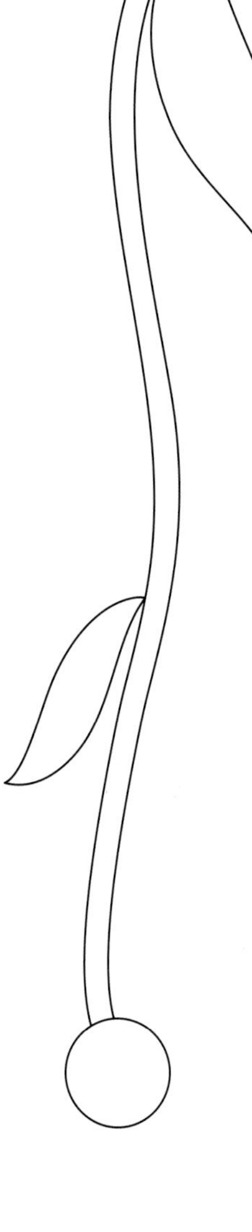

Block Appliqué Patterns
Enlarge 133%.

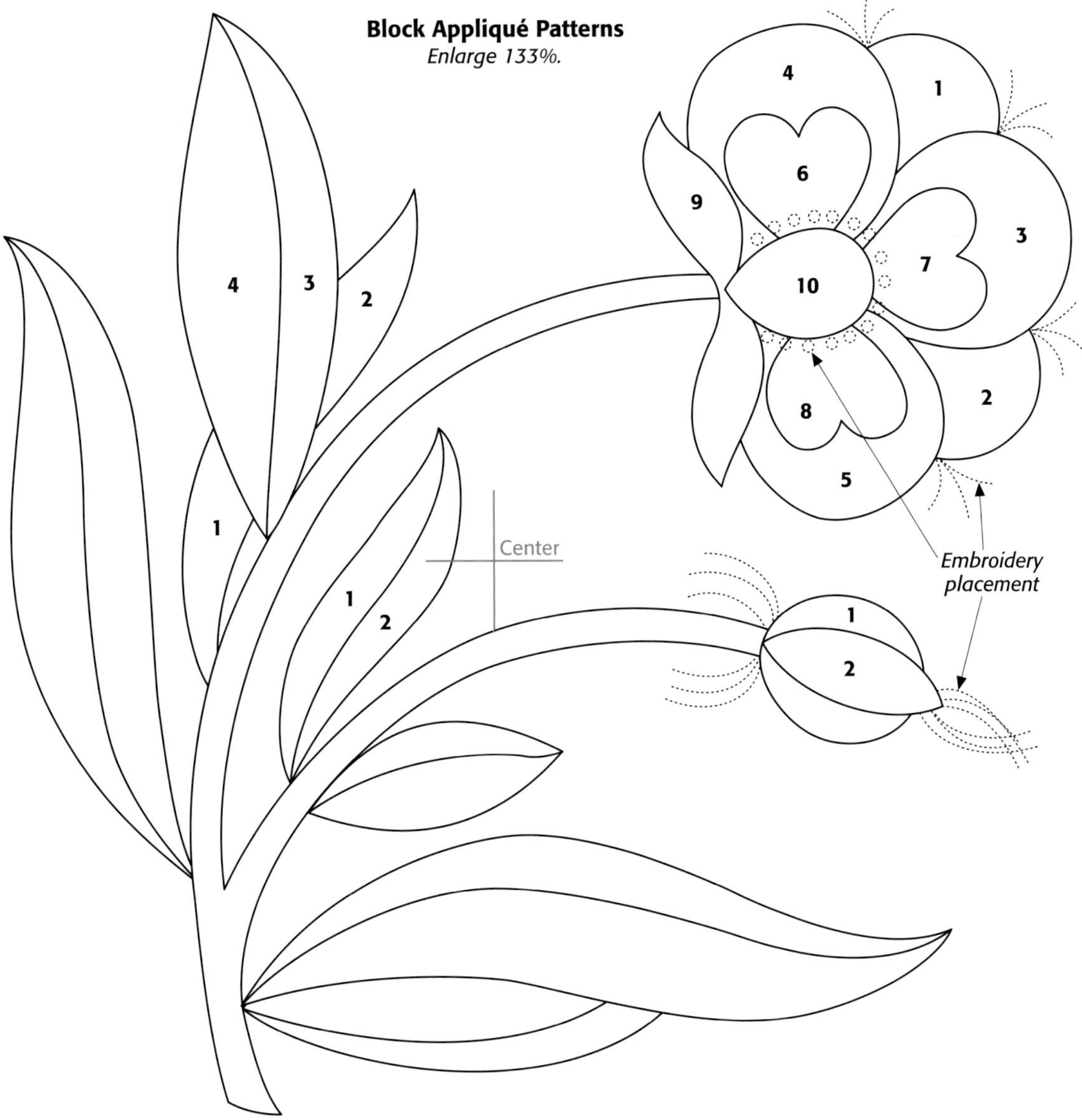

4

3

2

1

4

1

6

9

7

3

10

8

2

1

2

Center

5

Embroidery placement

1

2

Finished Quilt Size: 50" x 76" (125 cm x 190 cm) ▼ Finished Flying Geese Size: 2" x 4" (5 cm x 10 cm)

Anna's Quilt

Loved and immediately claimed by Karen Cunningham's daughter Anna, this traditional Flying Geese quilt would light up any room. ✿

Materials

Amounts are based on 42"-wide (107 cm) fabric.

- ▼ 2½ yards (2.2 m) of cream fabric for sky and third border
- ▼ 1¾ yards (1.5 m) of floral print for strip rows and first border
- ▼ ½ yard (40 cm) of pink fabric for second border
- ▼ 14 fat quarters **or** 28 fat eighths **or** 112 scraps of assorted fabrics for Flying Geese
- ▼ 3⅓ yards (3 m) of backing fabric
- ▼ ⅝ yard (50 cm) of binding fabric
- ▼ 54" x 80" (135 cm x 200 cm) piece of batting

Cutting

All cutting dimensions include ¼" seam allowances. Instructions are for cutting strips across the fabric width except where noted.

From the cream fabric, cut *lengthwise*:

- ▼ 2 strips, 6½" x 80"
- ▼ 2 strips, 6½" x 54"
- ▼ 5 strips, 2½" x 80"; crosscut into 160 squares, 2½" x 2½"

From the remaining cream, cut:

- ▼ 6 strips, 2½" wide; crosscut into 84 squares, 2½" x 2½"

From the assorted fabrics, cut:

- ▼ 8 rectangles, 2½" x 4½", from each fat quarter

or

- ▼ 4 rectangles, 2½" x 4½", from each fat eighth

or

- ▼ 112 rectangles, 2½" x 4½", from scraps

From the floral print, cut *lengthwise*:

- ▼ 5 strips, 4" x 56½"
- ▼ 1 strip, 4" x 34"

From the pink, cut:

- ▼ 6 strips, 2½" wide

From the binding fabric, cut:

- ▼ 7 strips, 2½" wide

Flying Geese Strips

1. On the wrong side of each of the 2½" cream squares, draw a diagonal line. Place one of the squares on one end of a 2½" x 4½" rectangle with right sides together. Stitch along the line, trim the excess fabric, leaving a ¼" seam allowance, and press the cream fabric toward the corner.

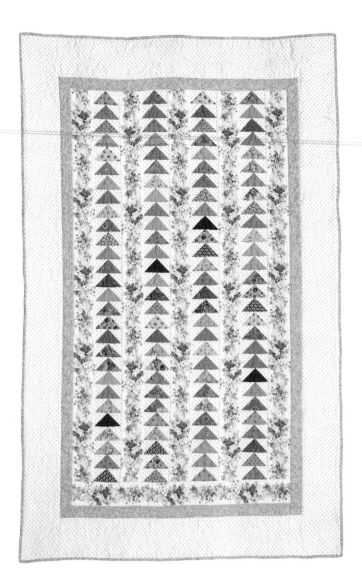

2. Repeat this process with another cream square at the other end of the rectangle. Note that the diagonal slants in the opposite direction on either end of the rectangle.

Make 112.

3. Sew the completed flying-geese units together along the long edges to form four rows of 28 Flying Geese. When sewing the flying-geese units together, make sure you stitch above the crossed lines of the stitching on the wrong side of each unit so you do not lose the points.

Quilt Assembly

1. Using the assembly diagram as a guide, lay out the four flying-geese strips and the five 56½"-long floral-print strips. Sew with the flying-geese strip on the top and use the previous stitching as a guide to ensure you do not lose the points of the geese. Sew the strips together, pressing the seams toward the floral print.

Make 4.

2. Sew the remaining (34"-long) floral-print strip to the bottom of the quilt. All the Flying Geese should point toward the top of the quilt.

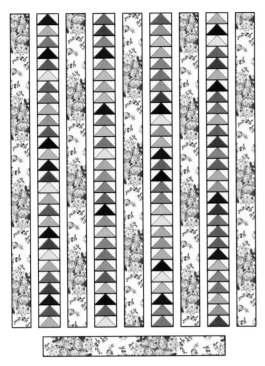

Assembly Diagram

Borders

1. Cut two of the pink strips to a length of 34". Sew these two strips to the top and bottom of the quilt and press toward the pink borders.

2. Sew the remaining four pink strips together in pairs, end to end. From each strip, cut a 64"-long strip. Sew these two strips to the sides of the quilt; press toward the pink borders.

3. The 6½"-wide cream border has mitered corners. Add the 80"-long strips to the sides of the quilt and the 54"-long strips to the top and bottom of the quilt according to "Borders with Mitered Corners" on page 106.

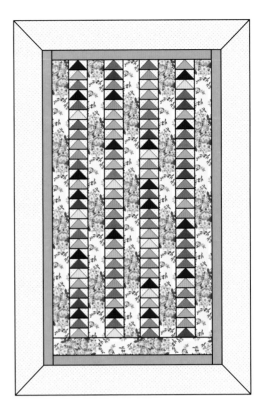

Finishing

1. Cut the backing fabric into two equal lengths and remove the selvages. Sew the two pieces together along the length to make a backing with a vertical seam; press the seam to one side.

2. Layer the backing, batting, and quilt top, smoothing each layer from the center outward as you go. Baste the three layers together, using your preferred method.

3. Hand or machine quilt as desired. "Anna's Quilt" was stipple quilted in the background of the Flying Geese, and a simple cable with four-patch intersections was quilted on the floral-print strips. The border was quilted with a continuous-line design.

4. Remove the basting and trim the excess batting and backing fabric even with the edges of the quilt top. Join the seven 2½"-wide binding strips end to end using angled seams; press the seams open. Attach the binding to the quilt, referring to "Finishing" on page 109 for more details.

5. Label your quilt, including your name, the date, and any other relevant information.

Finished Quilt Size: 42½" x 50½" (108 cm x 128 cm)

Springtime Daisies

This quilt, designed and made by talented South Australian quilter Tracey Browning, features bouquets of pretty daisies. A selection of spring greens and pastel pinks along with a wonderful floral fabric give this quilt its springtime feel. Tracey included hand-appliquéd flowers and leaves, embellishing them with easy embroidery stitches. Make your own version of this delightful quilt using your favorite springtime prints. 🌸

Materials

Amounts are based on 42"-wide (107 cm) fabric.

▼ 1⅝ yards (1.4 m) of floral print for triangles and borders

▼ ⅔ yard (60 cm) of pink check fabric for triangles

▼ ½ yard (50 cm) of green tone-on-tone print for center frame and binding

▼ ⅓ yard (30 cm) of green check fabric for center background

▼ Assorted pink, blue, and green fabric scraps for appliqué flowers and leaves

▼ 2¼ yards (2 m) of backing fabric

▼ 47" x 55" (120 cm x 140 cm) piece of batting

▼ Fusible web (optional)

▼ Embroidery thread to match appliqué fabrics

Cutting

All cutting dimensions include ¼" seam allowances. Instructions are for cutting strips across the fabric width.

From the green tone-on-tone print, cut:

▼ 2 strips, 2" wide; crosscut into 2 strips, 2" x 12½", and 2 strips, 2" x 11½"

▼ 5 binding strips, 2½" wide

From the green check, cut:

▼ 1 rectangle, 8½" x 12½"

From the floral print, cut:

▼ 5 strips, 6½" wide

▼ 4 strips, 2½" wide

▼ 1 rectangle, 12" x 16¼"

From the pink check, cut:

▼ 1 strip, 12¼" wide; crosscut 2 rectangles, 12¼" x 16¼"

▼ 4 strips, 2½" wide

Center Panel Assembly

1. Using a photocopy machine, enlarge the patterns on page 21 by 115%. Using the appliqué method of your choice, trace 19 daisy flowers and centers plus 38 leaves onto the assorted fabric scraps and cut them out.

2. Refer to the appliqué placement diagram to position the center cluster of seven flowers. Once all the pieces have been arranged, draw the stems where you want them to go. Be creative and different; flowers are not all uniform in the garden and need not be all the same in your quilt.

3. Using one strand of matching embroidery thread, blanket stitch around each appliqué piece. Using three strands of thread, stem stitch the stems over the pencil lines.

4. Sew a 12½"-long green tone-on-tone strip to the top and bottom of the green check rectangle and press the seams toward the strips. Sew the 11½"-long green tone-on-tone strips to both sides of the green check rectangle, again pressing the seams toward the strips.

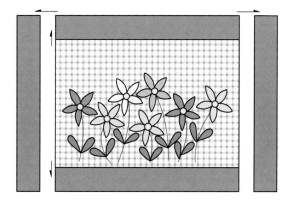

Quilt Assembly

1. Cut the 12" x 16¼" floral rectangle across both diagonals as shown to yield four triangles.

Fold the two longer triangles in half along the length and finger-press the fold. Fold and finger-press the middle of the long sides of the center panel. With right sides together and matching the folds, stitch the floral triangles to the center panel and press the seams toward the floral. There will be a ¼" overlap at each end. Fold, sew, and press the two remaining triangles as above.

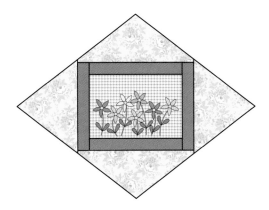

2. Place the two 12¼" x 16¼" pink check rectangles right sides together and cut them in half on the diagonal. Fold, sew, and press these triangles to the sides of the quilt top as above. Measure your quilt center and, if necessary, square it up to 22½" x 30½".

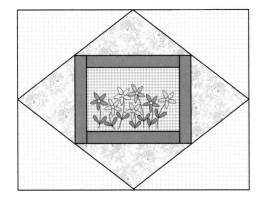

3. Place a group of three daisies in each of the pink check corners and appliqué as in step 3 of "Center Panel Assembly."

Borders

1. To make the checkered border, sew the 2½"-wide floral and pink check strips together lengthwise into pairs. Press the seams toward the floral strips and crosscut the strip sets into 60 segments, 2½" wide.

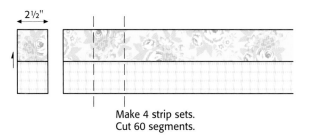

Make 4 strip sets.
Cut 60 segments.

Sew the segments together to make four checkered strips of 15 segments each.

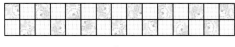

Make 4.

Sew a checkered border strip to the top and bottom of the quilt top, orienting the strip so that the floral squares on each end of the strip lie next to the quilt top as shown. Press the seams toward the center of the quilt top. Join the two remaining borders to each side of the quilt top, again placing them so that the end floral squares are next to the quilt top to ensure that the checkered effect continues around the border. Press toward the center.

2. For the floral border, trim two of the 6½"-wide floral-print strips to 38½" long. Sew these strips to the top and bottom edges of the quilt top. Press the seams toward the borders. Sew the remaining three 6½"-wide floral-print strips together end to end, and from this piece, cut two strips 42½" long. Sew these strips to the sides of the quilt and press the seams toward the borders.

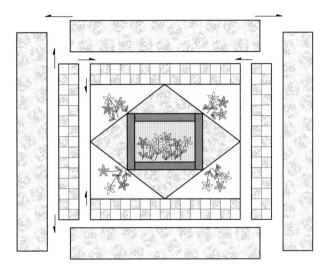

Finishing

1. Cut one 55" piece and two 10" pieces across the width of your backing fabric. Sew the two 10" pieces end to end and trim this piece to 55" long. Sew this piece to the large piece along the length to make a back that is approximately 48" x 55".

2. Layer the backing, batting, and quilt top, smoothing each layer from the center outward as you go. Baste the three layers together using your preferred method.

3. Hand or machine quilt as desired. Tracey's quilt was machine quilted. She outlined each of the daisies and added quilted "grass" to the center cluster. The floral triangles and border were quilted with a pattern of swirling leaves and tendrils, and the pink background, including all the pink squares in the checkered border, were stipple quilted.

4. Remove the basting and trim the excess batting and backing fabric even with the edges of the quilt top. Join the five 2½"-wide binding strips end to end using angled seams; press the seams open. Attach the binding to the quilt, referring to "Finishing" on page 109 for more details.

5. Label your quilt, including your name, the date, and any other relevant information.

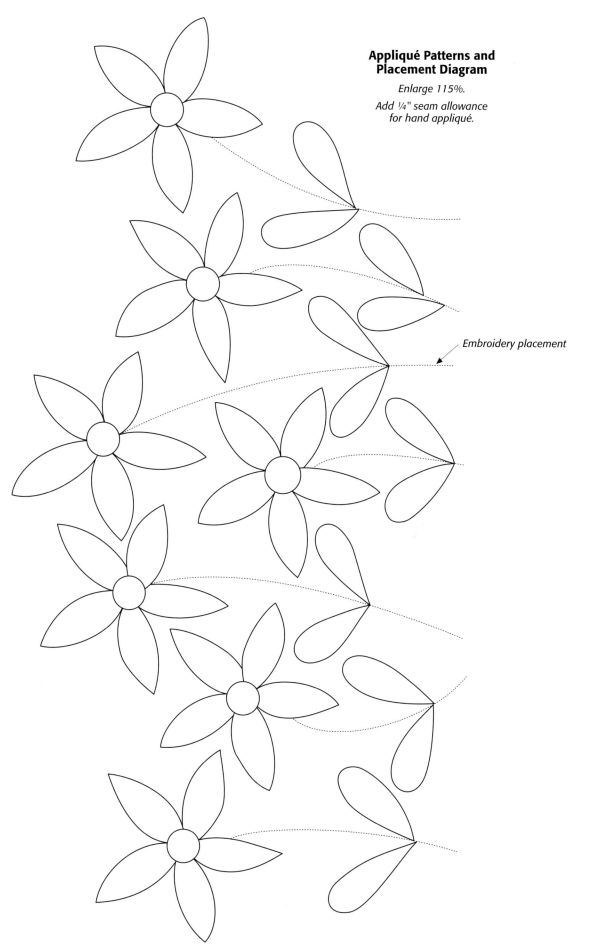

Appliqué Patterns and Placement Diagram

Enlarge 115%.

Add ¼" seam allowance for hand appliqué.

Embroidery placement

Finished Quilt Size: 77½" x 82" (196 cm x 205 cm)

STARRY, STARRY NIGHT

"Starry, Starry Night" was a project Sheila Bennett worked on in her spare time and an opportunity for her to use fabrics from her vast array of floral scraps. Sheila constructed her quilt using the paper-piecing method. Because the technique involves working with one piece at a time, she was able to pack a little sewing bag wherever she went and bring it out when she had a few spare moments. "Starry, Starry Night" is a soft, pretty quilt, but you may find that your scrap collection is of an entirely different nature! 🌹

Materials

Amounts are based on 42"-wide (107 cm) fabric.

- ▼ Assorted floral fabrics for stars
- ▼ 4 yards (3.6 m) of light fabric for background
- ▼ 2⅜ yards (2.2 m) of pink fabric for border
- ▼ 5 yards (4.5 m) of backing fabric
- ▼ ¾ yard (70 cm) of binding fabric
- ▼ 82" x 86" (220 cm x 225 cm) piece of batting
- ▼ Template plastic
- ▼ Card stock or sturdy paper, or precut paper shapes: 1½" (4 cm) 60-degree diamond and 1½" (4 cm) hexagon

Fabric Selection

Sheila used a different fabric for every star in the quilt. The minimum amount needed for each star is a 7" (18 cm) square. If you use fat quarters for your assortment, you can get four stars from each fat quarter, plus a few of the extra diamonds. Enjoy working with your own scrap fabrics, whatever you have. This will be a stunning quilt in any color combination.

Cutting

All cutting dimensions include ¼" seam allowances. Instructions are for cutting strips across the fabric width except where noted.

From the light fabric, cut:

- ▼ 34 strips, 3½" wide; crosscut into 432 rectangles, 3" x 3½"

From the pink fabric, cut *lengthwise*:

- ▼ 4 strips, 6" wide

From the binding fabric, cut:

- ▼ 8 strips, 2½" wide

Preparation

1. Trace the diamond and hexagon patterns from page 27 onto the template plastic. Cut them out accurately.

2. Trace the required quantity of shapes onto the card stock or paper. You will need 1,284 diamonds and 432 hexagons. It is important that you cut the shapes out on the inside of the pencil lines to maintain accuracy. You may skip this step if you have purchased the precut paper shapes.

Stars

There is a total of 203 stars, 26 pairs of diamonds, and 14 single diamonds required for this quilt.

1. For each star, place and pin six paper diamonds to the wrong side of the fabric, leaving room between each diamond for the seam allowances. Cut the fabric ¼" larger than the paper shapes. Prepare the paired and single diamonds in the same manner. Fold the ¼" seam allowance over the paper and baste into position as shown, then press the shapes.

2. Place two diamonds right sides together and join them along one side using a small whip-stitch, just catching the edges of the fabric. When sewing the pieces together, use a good-quality thread. Sheila prefers to use a single strand of quilting thread or a double strand of cotton thread.

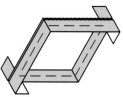

3. Continue joining the diamonds until you have a star. The seam allowances will nest into each other on the wrong side when sewn together.

The nested seams will also help to reduce bulk in places where many seams come together, such as the center points of the stars. Construct the stars and the pairs of diamonds in this manner.

Hexagons

1. Place and pin the paper hexagon shapes on the light (background) rectangles and trim the seam allowance to ¼".

2. Fold the ¼" seam allowance over the paper and baste into position as shown, then press the shapes.

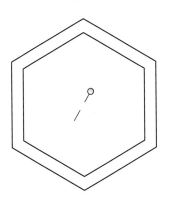
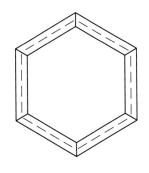

Quilt Assembly

The quilt is assembled in two row variations.

1. The first row has 14 stars and 26 hexagons. Sew a hexagon to the first star and sew another hexagon to the same star as shown. Sew the next star to the two hexagons, and continue on down the row in the same manner, ending with a star. Sew the pieces together using the whipstitch method in step 2 on page 24. Join all the required pieces and make eight strips of row 1 as shown.

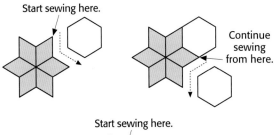

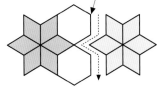

Row 1
Make 8.

2. The second row has 13 stars and 28 hexagons. Sew a hexagon to the first star and sew another hexagon to the same star as shown. Continue on down the row as in step 1 but end with two hexagons. Join all the required pieces and make seven strips of row 2 as shown.

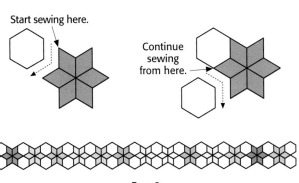

Row 2
Make 7.

Sew a single diamond to both ends of each row 2 to complete the design.

3. Sew the rows together to form the main body of the quilt.

   Note: The quilt will be lighter and easier to work with if you occasionally remove some of the paper pieces. You may remove the paper at any time as long as all the edges of a particular piece have been sewn to another piece. This means that you won't be able to remove paper at the edges of the quilt until after the pieces have been sewn to the border strips. Simply remove the basting and pull out each paper piece.

4. For the top and bottom of the quilt, sew a row of single hexagons joined by pairs of diamonds to complete the design. Refer to the assembly diagram for placement.

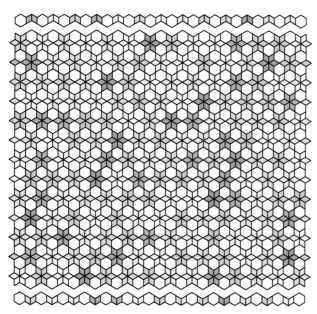

Assembly Diagram

Border

1. Fold each border strip in half crosswise and crease lightly to mark the centers. Aligning centers, place one of the border strips along a side of the quilt top, extending the border 5¼" past the star points. Pin the center in place. Approximately ¾" of the border strip will be under the quilt top. Pin the entire side to the border strip at intervals, making sure that 5¼" of the border extends past the star points.

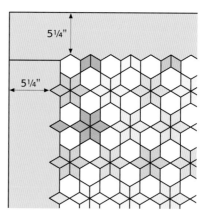

2. Appliqué the side of the quilt to the border, leaving the first and last hexagons unstitched to allow access for the other border strips. Appliqué the opposite side in the same manner.

3. Appliqué the top and bottom edges of the quilt to the remaining border strips as you did for the sides.

4. To join the borders at the corner, fold under the seam allowance on one strip and appliqué it on top of the underlying strip. Trim the excess fabric from the seam allowance. Repeat this on the remaining three corners. Complete the appliqué of the hexagons at the corners and remove the paper pieces.

Finishing

1. Cut the backing fabric into two equal lengths and remove the selvages. Sew the two pieces together along the length to make a backing with a vertical seam; press the seam to one side.

2. Layer the backing, batting, and quilt top, smoothing each layer from the center outward as you go. Baste the three layers together using your preferred method.

3. Hand or machine quilt as desired. This quilt was hand quilted. Each hexagon was echo quilted ⅜" inside the seam lines, forming a smaller hexagon pattern. Diagonal lines were quilted in both directions, following the edges of the hexagons and continuing along and through the stars. This formed a quilted hexagon within each of the stars. A petal design was used to complete the borders.

4. Remove the basting and trim the excess batting and backing fabric even with the edges of the quilt top. To make the rounded corners, place a round object, such as a plate, at the edge of each corner and trace with a pencil. Cut away the three layers of the quilt.

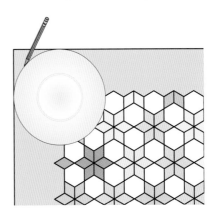

5. Join the eight 2½"-wide binding strips end to end using angled seams; press the seams open. Attach the binding to the quilt, referring to "Finishing" on page 109 for more details.

6. Label your quilt, including your name, the date, and any other relevant information.

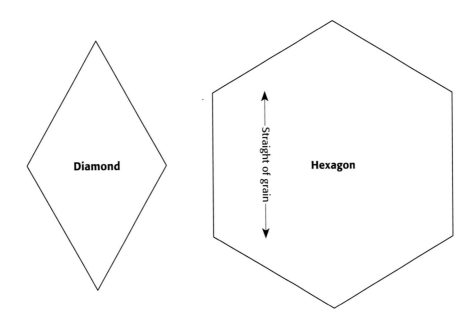

Diamond

Straight of grain

Hexagon

Finished Quilt Size: 72½" x 84" (182 cm x 210 cm) ▼ Finished Block Size: 3½" x 3½" (9 cm x 9 cm)

PRETTY STRIPPY

This lovely strip quilt by Joy White is certainly pretty in pink! The richness of the fabrics combine with beautiful quilting in dark pink thread to make it particularly eye-catching. It's a simple quilt to make—all machine pieced and quilted. 🌹

Materials

Amounts are based on 42"-wide (107 cm) fabric.

▼ 3¼ yards (2.8 m) of mushroom pink floral print for wide strips, blocks, and main border

▼ 2¼ yards (2 m) of light pink solid fabric for wide strips and four-patch-strip background

▼ 2 yards (1.8 m) of dark pink tone-on-tone print for narrow strips, blocks, and binding

▼ 5 yards (4.5 m) of backing fabric

▼ 78" x 88" (200 cm x 230 cm) piece of batting

Cutting

All cutting dimensions include ¼" seam allowances. Instructions are for cutting strips across the fabric width except where noted.

From the mushroom pink floral print, cut:

▼ 14 strips, 2¼" wide; crosscut 7 strips into 104 squares, 2¼" x 2¼"

From the remaining *length* of mushroom pink floral print, cut:

▼ 6 strips, 6½" wide

▼ 4 squares, 3¾" x 3¾"

From the dark pink tone-on-tone print, cut:

▼ 7 strips, 2¼" wide

▼ 24 strips, 1½" wide

▼ 8 binding strips, 2" wide

From the light pink solid fabric, cut *lengthwise*:

▼ 3 strips, 6½" wide

▼ 3 strips, 3¾" wide; crosscut into 52 squares 3¾" x 3¾"; cut squares twice diagonally to yield 208 quarter-square triangles

From the remaining light pink solid, cut:

▼ 4 squares, 3¾" x 3¾"

Four-Patch Units

1. Pair the seven 2¼"-wide floral strips with the seven 2¼"-wide dark pink strips and sew them together along the length of the strips. Press the seams toward the dark pink. Crosscut the strip sets into 2¼"-wide segments.

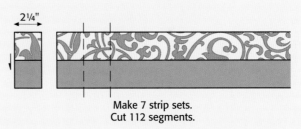

Make 7 strip sets.
Cut 112 segments.

2. Sew the segments together into four-patch units, carefully matching the seams.

Make 56.

29

Setting Units

1. Place a light pink triangle over a 2¼" floral square, with right sides together and the right-angle corners carefully aligned as shown. Sew the triangle to the square and press the seam toward the triangle.

2. Place another light pink triangle over the pieces just sewn, with this triangle's right-angle corner at the opposite corner of the square. Sew and press the seam toward the triangle.

Make 104.

End Units

1. Draw a diagonal line on the four 3¾" light pink squares. Place them right sides together with the four 3¾" floral squares and sew ¼" from either side of the pencil line. Cut along the pencil line and press the seam toward the floral fabric. Cut each square in half diagonally.

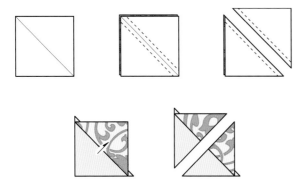

2. To construct each end unit, you will need one four-patch unit, one setting unit, and two units from step 1. Sew a setting unit to one side of a four-patch unit, carefully placing the floral square as shown. Sew each unit from step 1 to the four-patch unit, one at a time, as shown.

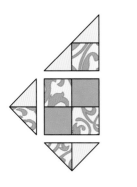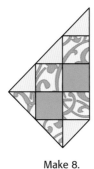

Make 8.

Pieced Strip Assembly

1. Sew a setting unit to opposite sides of the four-patch units, carefully placing the floral squares as shown.

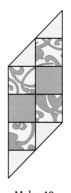

Make 48.

2. Sew 12 of these units together so that the dark pink squares match point to point and form a line down the center of the strip. Accurately match the seams and the light pink triangles; join end to end to form the straight edges of the strips. Carefully press the seams in one direction, ensuring you do not stretch the strip. Repeat with the remaining 36 units to make three more strips.

3. Sew an end unit to each end of the strips and press each seam in the direction of the other seams.

Make 4.

Quilt Assembly

1. Place the pieced strips on a flat surface and measure their length; they should measure 70". If they are not 70", adjust the length of the following strips to match the actual length of your pieced strips.

2. Sew 20 of the 1½"-wide dark pink strips together in pairs, end to end. From each of these 10 strips, cut a 70" length.

3. Trim two 6½"-wide floral strips and three 6½"-wide light pink strips to a length of 70".

4. Place a dark pink strip and a pieced strip right sides together, raw edges aligned, and pin the strips, easing to fit. Sew the strips together. When stitching a fabric strip to a pieced strip, stitch with the pieced strip on top and use the points of the Four Patch blocks as your stitching line. Stitch another dark pink strip to the other side in the same manner. Repeat this step for each of the pieced strips and press the seams toward the dark pink strips.

5. Sew a dark pink-plus-pieced strip to either side of a 6½"-wide floral strip; press toward the floral strip. Sew one light pink strip between the pieced strips as shown at right. If the floral prints are directional, check to ensure they are both facing the right way. Press toward the light pink strip.

6. Sew a light pink strip to either side of this large piece and press toward the light pink strips. Sew a 1½"-wide dark pink strip to either side of this large piece; press toward the dark pink strips.

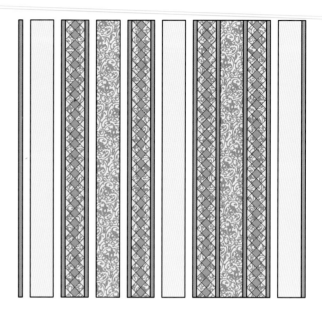

Borders

1. Measure the width of the quilt top through the center; it should measure 60½".

2. Sew the remaining four 1½"-wide dark pink strips together in pairs, end to end. From each of these two strips, cut a 60½" length. Sew these strips to the top and bottom edges of the quilt top. Press toward the dark pink strips.

3. Measure the length of the quilt top through the center; it should measure 72". Trim two of the 6½"-wide floral strips to this measurement. Sew these strips to the sides of the quilt top and press the seams toward the borders. Measure the width of the quilt top through the center; it should now measure 72½". Trim the two remaining 6½"-wide floral strips to this measurement. Sew these strips to the top and bottom edges of the quilt top. Press the seams toward the borders.

Finishing

1. Cut the backing fabric into two equal lengths, remove the selvages, and sew the two pieces together along the length to make a backing with a vertical seam. Press the seam to one side.

2. Layer the backing, batting, and quilt top, smoothing each layer from the center outward as you go. Baste the three layers together using your preferred method.

3. Hand or machine quilt as desired. Joy's quilt was beautifully machine quilted by Deborah Louis on her domestic machine. Deborah quilted a floral pattern in the solid pink strips using a dark pink quilting thread. She outline quilted the pieced strips and chose a simple design for the floral panels and border.

4. Remove the basting and trim the excess batting and backing fabric even with the edges of the quilt top. Join the eight 2"-wide binding strips end to end using angled seams; press the seams open. Attach the binding to the quilt, referring to "Finishing" on page 109 for more details.

5. Label your quilt, including your name, the date, and any other relevant information.

Finished Quilt Size: 85½" x 98½" (217 cm x 250 cm) ▼ Finished Block Size: 20" x 20" (51 cm x 51 cm)

Hearts and Roses

Tricia Sewell based the central design of this quilt on an American quilt that appeared in the background of a newspaper photograph she came across years ago. She set about designing the center, using special fabrics that she had been collecting. As for the rest of it, Tricia says, "Like a lot of my quilts, the borders just evolved as I went along. The final design has a very traditional look, which I particularly enjoy."

Materials

Amounts are based on 42"-wide (107 cm) fabric.

- ▼ 3¾ yards (3.4 m) of green floral print for sashing, pieced border, and fifth border
- ▼ 3½ yards (3 m) of green background print for appliqué border and pieced border
- ▼ 2¾ yards (2.5 m) of beige tone-on-tone print for block background and cornerstones
- ▼ 1¾ yards (1.5 m) of green stripe fabric for first and third borders, appliqué vine, and binding
- ▼ 1¼ yards (1.1 m) of red check fabric for star points
- ▼ ⅝ yard (60 cm) of yellow accent print for appliqué stars and hearts in blocks
- ▼ ⅜ yard (40 cm) *each* of 3 red and 3 green prints for appliqué in block centers and appliqué border
- ▼ ¼ yard (20 cm) *each* of 5 green and 5 yellow prints for appliqué border
- ▼ 8 yards (7.2 m) of backing fabric
- ▼ 90" x 103" (225 cm x 260 cm) piece of batting

Cutting

All cutting dimensions include ¼" seam allowances. Instructions are for cutting strips across the fabric width except where noted.

From the beige tone-on-tone print, cut:

- ▼ 6 squares, 14" x 14"
- ▼ 3 strips, 4½" wide; crosscut into 24 squares, 4½" x 4½", **or** cut 24 of template A
- ▼ 2 strips, 3½" wide; crosscut into 24 squares, 3½" x 3½", **or** cut 24 of template B
- ▼ 24 of template C
- ▼ 6 of template P

From the red check, cut:

- ▼ 24 of template D
- ▼ 24 of template DR

From the yellow accent print, cut:

- ▼ 24 of template E
- ▼ 24 of template F

From *each* of the ⅜-yard pieces of red and green prints, cut:

- ▼ 1 of template G
- ▼ 4 of template H

From 1 of the remaining red prints, cut:

- ▼ 24 of template I

From the remaining red prints, cut:

▼ 28 of template N

▼ 24 of template P

▼ 12 of template I

▼ 48 rectangles, 1½" x 2½"

From 1 of the remaining green prints, cut:

▼ 2 of template E

From the ¼-yard pieces of 5 green prints, cut a total of:

▼ 24 of template L

▼ 24 of template M

▼ 20 of template Q

▼ 20 of template R

From the ¼-yard pieces of 5 yellow prints, cut a total of:

▼ 12 of template F

▼ 28 of template I

▼ 120 of template O (in sets of 5)

From the green stripe, cut:

▼ 16 strips, 1" wide

▼ 10 strips, 2¼" wide

▼ 12 bias strips, 1" wide

▼ 2 bias strips, ¾" wide

From the green background print, cut lengthwise:

▼ 2 strips, 9½" x 72"

▼ 2 strips, 9½" x 95"

▼ 16 of template J

From the green floral print, cut *lengthwise:*

▼ 2 strips, 3½" x 89"

▼ 2 strips, 3½" x 102"

From the remaining green floral print, cut:

▼ 17 strips, 3½" x 20½"

▼ 14 of template J

▼ 2 of template K

▼ 2 of template KR

Appliqué Preparation

Trace all of the patterns on pages 43–46 onto template plastic (except for patterns I and P, which should be traced onto cardboard because you'll be pressing fabric while it's on the templates). Label the templates and carefully cut them out on the drawn lines. Add a seam allowance when cutting out fabric for hand appliqué. No seam allowances are needed for fusible web. Refer to "Cutting" on page 35 for the number to cut of each shape.

Templates C and J are half patterns. Place the template on fabric that has been folded in half, right side out, and trace the design. Then open the fabric, right side up, and align the template with the other half of the fabric. Connecting with the lines you just drew, trace the other half. Template G is one-quarter of the pattern required. Fold the fabric into quarters, right side out, and finger-press the folds. Open the fabric, right side up, and use the creases to center the design in each quarter and trace.

Block Assembly

1. Fold the 14" beige background squares into halves, then quarters, and finally into triangles. Gently press the folds and open them out. Baste or pin a pattern G piece to each of the background squares, lining up the center of the hearts with the diagonal fold lines. Be sure that the stitching lines are at least ½" from the raw edges. Place four pattern H pieces 3" from the center of each block as

shown and baste or pin them in position. Appliqué the pieces in place, using thread to match the fabrics.

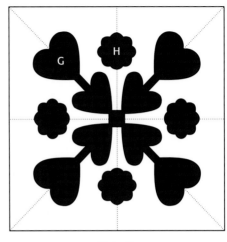

Make 6.

2. Cut away the center of the pattern H pieces, leaving a ⅛" seam allowance; be careful you don't cut the background fabric. Appliqué the inside of the circles. Stitch a gathering line within the seam allowance of the circles you cut away, and center cardboard template I on the wrong side of one circle. Gently pull up the threads to form a smooth circle and press it well. Once it is cool, remove the cardboard template and appliqué the circle into place. Continue with the remaining 23 circles.

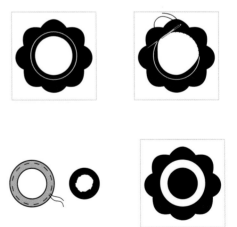

3. Prepare the six beige pattern P circles, using the cardboard template as in step 2. Appliqué one to the center of each heart G design.

4. Using a square ruler, trim the block to 12½" square, taking care to keep the appliqué design centered.

5. Center a yellow pattern E heart on each of the pattern C triangles as shown. Baste or pin them in place and appliqué them in the same manner as before. Stitch pattern D and DR triangles to each side of the appliquéd C pieces.

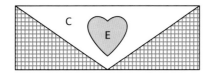

Make 24.

6. Center and baste or pin each of the 24 yellow pattern F star flowers onto the 4½" background squares. Appliqué the flowers in place. Sew a gathering stitch around each of the red pattern I pieces and, using the cardboard template as in step 2, make 24 red centers. Appliqué a red center to each of the star flowers.

Make 24.

7. Sew a completed D/C/DR rectangle to the top and bottom of each of the six appliquéd center squares. Sew a 4½" appliquéd square to either end of the remaining D/C/DR rectangles. Stitch these strips to the opposite sides of each of the appliquéd center squares, carefully matching the seam intersections as you go.

Make 6.

Quilt Center Assembly

1. Using the assembly diagram as a guide, lay out the six blocks in three rows of two blocks each, with the 3½" x 20½" green floral sashing strips and 3½" beige cornerstones between the blocks.

2. Stitch four rows of three cornerstones and two sashing strips and press the seams toward the sashing strips. Sew the blocks together in rows, starting and ending each one with a sashing strip, and press the seams toward the sashing strips.

3. Join the completed rows together, carefully matching the intersections. Appliqué a pattern E heart on each of the two center cornerstones. The center section of the quilt top should now measure 49½" x 72½".

Assembly Diagram

First Border

1. Join seven of the 1"-wide green stripe strips into one length, taking care to match the design as you go. From this length, cut two 54"-long strips and two 77"-long strips.

2. This green stripe border has mitered corners. Sew the 54"-long strips to the top and bottom of the quilt top and the 77"-long strips to the sides according to "Borders with Mitered Corners" on page 106. The quilt top should now measure 50½" x 73½".

Note: The first, second, and third borders can be sewn to the quilt as a unit. Refer to the note in "Borders with Mitered Corners" on page 106.

Second (Appliqué) Border

1. This border has mitered corners as well. Sew the 72"-long green background border strips to the top and bottom of the quilt top and the 95"-long strips to the sides as in step 2 of the first border. The quilt top should now measure 68½" x 91½".

2. To make the vines, sew the 1"-wide bias strips together with diagonal seams to make four lengths 26½" long and eight lengths 21½" long. Fold these strips in half lengthwise with wrong sides together and stitch a ⅛" seam along the length to form a tube.

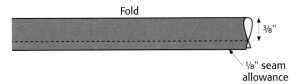

Fold

⅜"

⅛" seam allowance

Press the vines so the seam is off-center at the back of the tube, ensuring the raw edges do not protrude at the sides.

Using the appliqué placement diagrams on page 47 as a guide, pin the vines into place. (For a full-size layout, enlarge the diagrams 400%.) Use the longer strips to go around the corners and the shorter strips for the central sections.

3. Tricia used the rolled-bias-stem technique to achieve her narrow stems that connect some of the leaves and flowers to the vine. Fold the ¾"-wide bias strips wrong sides together and sew along the length ⅛" from the folded edge.

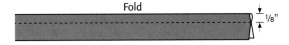

Fold

⅛"

Trim the seam allowance to ⅛"; roll the folded edge over the stitching and slip-stitch.

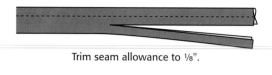

Trim seam allowance to ⅛".

Roll folded edge over stitching and slip-stitch.

Trim the leaf and flower stems to the desired lengths from the long bias strips and pin them in place on the border. Appliqué the stems, tucking one raw end under the vine. The flowers and leaves will cover the other raw end of each stem.

4. Appliqué the vines. The flowers and leaves will cover the raw ends of the vines.

5. The L and M leaves have reverse-appliqué centers. Place a 1½" x 2½" rectangle of red fabric with the right side facing the wrong side of each of the 24 pattern L leaves and pin. On the right side of each leaf, lightly trace template S as shown, making sure it is entirely within the area covered by the red fabric. Carefully cut away the leaf fabric only inside of this drawn line, leaving a ⅛" seam allowance. Appliqué along the drawn line, turning under the seam allowance as you go.

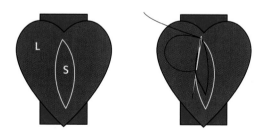

Trim the excess red fabric from behind the leaf. Stitch these completed leaves to each end of the border vines. Again using template S, reverse appliqué each of the 24 pattern M leaves in the same manner and then stitch them in place.

6. Make the remaining leaves from patterns Q and R. Stitch the R shape to the Q piece, and then appliqué the completed leaf in place on the border.

7. Prepare the 12 red pattern I flower centers, using the cardboard template as in step 2 of "Block Assembly," and add them to the center of the yellow star flowers. Appliqué the completed flowers in place on the border. Prepare the 28 yellow pattern I flower centers in the same way and add them to the center of the pattern N flowers. Appliqué these completed flowers onto the border.

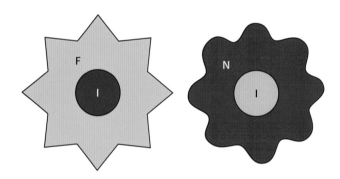

8. To make the five-petal flowers, appliqué the pattern O petals in position one at a time, overlapping the edges as you go. For more perfect-looking circles, you may wish to make a cardboard template O and prepare the 120 yellow flower petals in the same way as the flower centers in step 7. Prepare the 24 red pattern P flower centers as in step 7 and appliqué them in the center of each of the five-petal flowers.

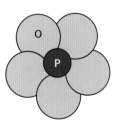

Third Border

1. Join the remaining nine 1"-wide green stripe strips into one length, taking care to match the design as you go. From this length, cut two 73"-long strips for the top and bottom borders and two 96"-long strips for the side borders.

2. Sew these strips to the quilt top as in step 2 of "First Border" to make a border with mitered corners. The quilt top should now measure 69½" x 92½".

Fourth (Pieced) Border

This border of pieced triangles is added only to the sides of the quilt top.

1. Sew the pattern J triangles together as shown to form two strips of eight green background triangles and seven green floral triangles. Stitch a pattern K to one end and a KR to the other end to complete the strips.

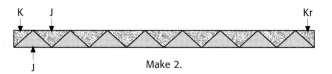

Make 2.

2. Sew the borders to the sides of the quilt top, with the green background triangles next to the third border. The quilt top should now measure 79½" x 92½".

Fifth Border

Sew the 89"-long green floral border strips to the top and bottom of the quilt top, and the 102"-long strips to the sides as in step 2 of "First Border" to make a border with mitered corners. The completed quilt top should now measure 85½" x 98½".

Finishing

1. Cut the backing fabric into three 90" lengths, remove the selvages, and sew the three pieces together along the length to make a pieced back with two horizontal seams. Press the seams to one side. You may wish to trim the length of the back to 103".

2. Layer the backing, batting, and quilt top, smoothing each layer from the center outward as you go. Baste the three layers together using your preferred method.

3. Hand or machine quilt as desired. The featured quilt was hand quilted with outline quilting to enhance the appliqué, then echo quilted every ¼" in the appliqué section of the blocks. A small motif was quilted on either side of the hearts in the blocks, and each of the print triangles was quilted ¼" and ½" from the seam line. The corner stars were echo quilted and hearts were quilted in the cornerstones. The sashing strips were quilted with a simple cable design. The appliqué border was quilted in a 2" grid, the triangles were repeated in the quilting in the pieced border, and the fifth border was quilted with a diagonal line of stitching.

4. Remove the basting and trim the excess batting and backing fabric even with the edges of the quilt top. Join the ten 2¼"-wide binding strips end to end using angled seams; press the seams open. Attach the binding to the quilt, referring to "Finishing" on page 109 for details.

5. Label your quilt, including your name, the date, and any other relevant information.

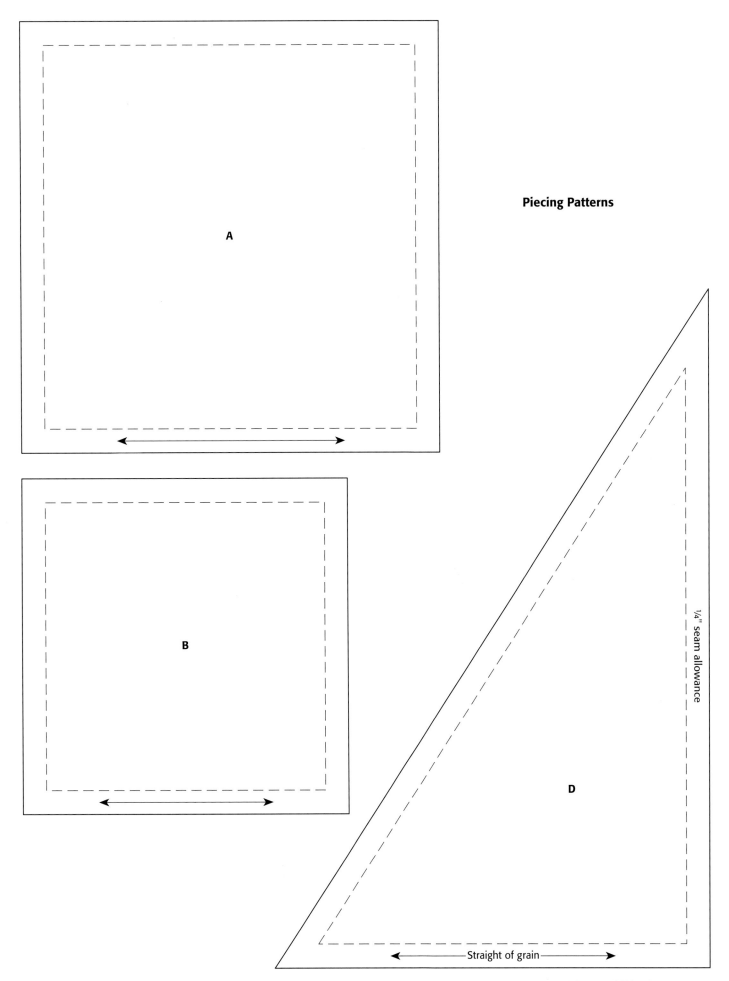

Piecing Patterns

A

B

D

¼" seam allowance

Straight of grain

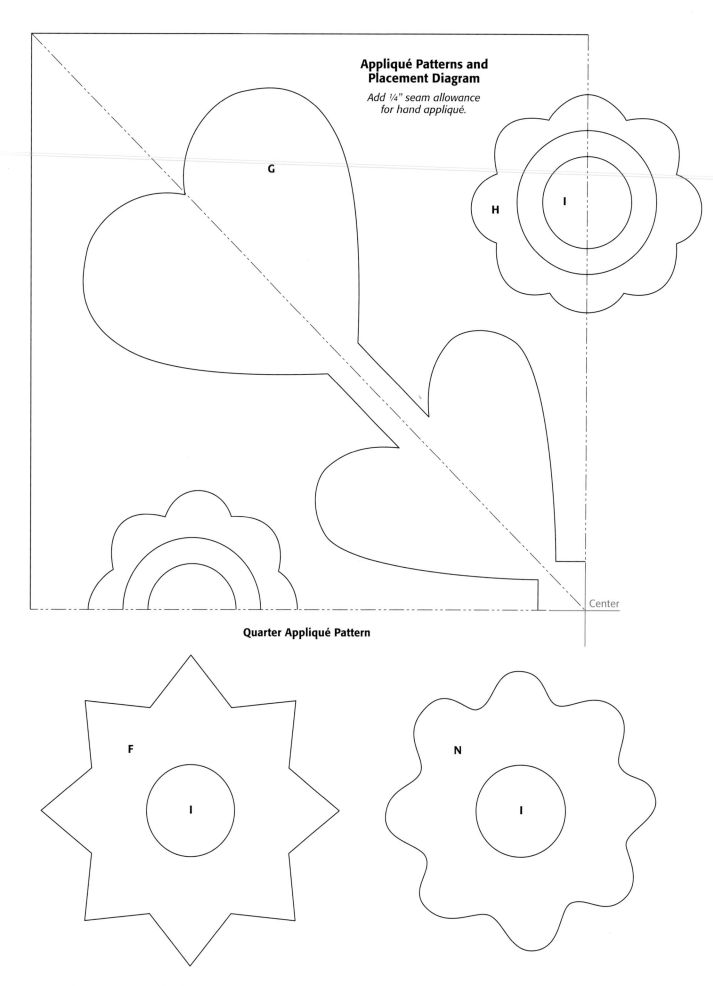

Appliqué Patterns and Placement Diagram

Add ¼" seam allowance for hand appliqué.

G

H

I

Center

Quarter Appliqué Pattern

F

I

N

I

Piecing and Appliqué Patterns

*Add ¼" seam allowance
for hand appliqué.*

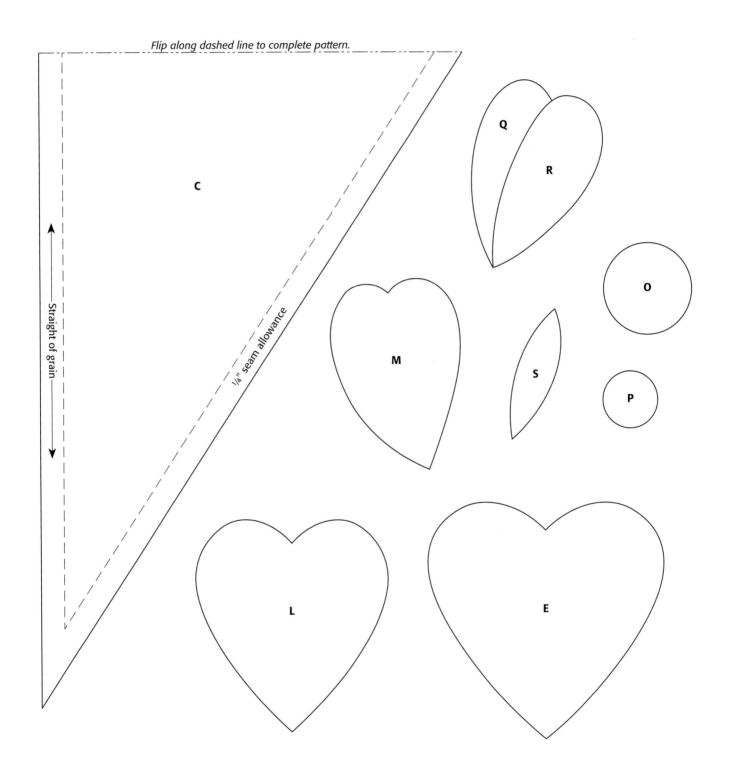

Flip along dashed line to complete pattern.

C

Straight of grain

¼" seam allowance

Q

R

O

M

S

P

L

E

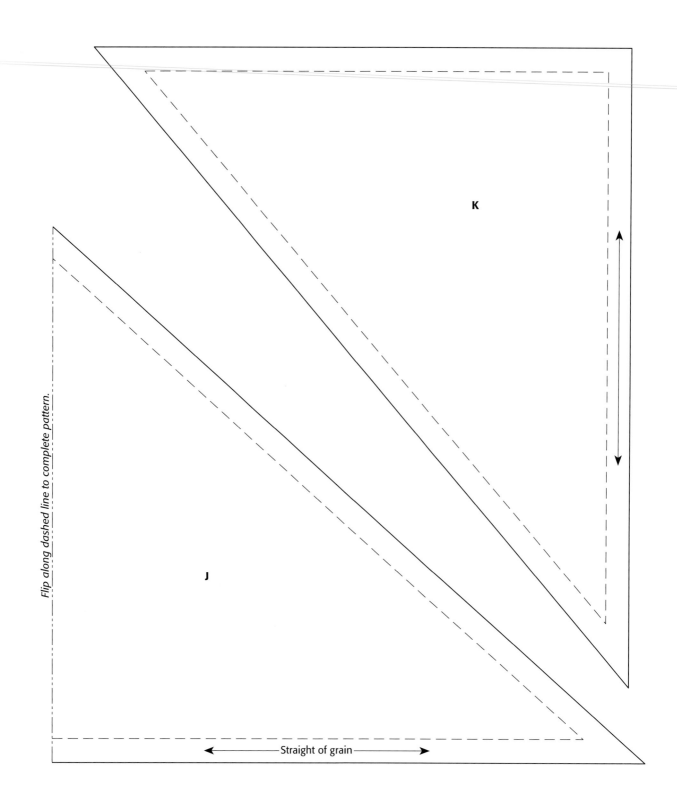

K

J

Flip along dashed line to complete pattern.

←——— Straight of grain ———→

Appliqué Border Placement Diagram
Enlarge 400%.

Fold

Align with dashed line.

Align with dashed line.

Finished Quilt Size: 43" x 20" (109 cm x 51 cm)

Midsummer Blooms

An array of earth-tone and cream fabrics was collected by Coral Smith for this beautiful wall hanging. This impressive quilt would be a lovely accent in any home. 🌸

Materials

Amounts are based on 42"-wide (107 cm) fabric.

- ▼ 1⅓ yards (120 cm) of beige tone-on-tone print for background and backing
- ▼ ½ yard (40 cm) of medium brown print for second border and binding
- ▼ ¼ yard (20 cm) of dark brown print for first border
- ▼ 1 fat quarter of green print for appliqué stems
- ▼ Scraps of brown prints for flowers (Coral used 7.)
- ▼ Scraps of green prints for leaves (Coral used 4.)
- ▼ 7" x 8" (18 cm x 20 cm) scrap of brown print for vase
- ▼ 47" x 24" (120 cm x 60 cm) piece of batting
- ▼ Fusible web (optional)
- ▼ ¼" (6 mm) bias pressing bar (optional)
- ▼ Spray starch (optional)

Cutting

All cutting dimensions include ¼" seam allowances. Instructions are for cutting strips across the fabric width except where noted.

From the beige tone-on-tone print, cut *lengthwise*:

- ▼ 1 rectangle, 18" x 41", for background (Use the remaining 22"-wide piece for backing.)

From the dark brown print, cut:

- ▼ 4 strips, 1" wide

From the medium brown print, cut:

- ▼ 4 strips, 1½" wide
- ▼ 4 binding strips, 2½" wide

Appliqué

1. Fold the beige (background) rectangle in half both horizontally and vertically and crease the folds lightly or mark them with large basting stitches to act as a guide for the design placement. Lightly trace the design onto the background fabric, using the appliqué placement guide on page 55, or enlarge the diagram 400% for a full-size layout.

2. Make the stems, using one of the following methods.

For hand appliqué: From the green print fat quarter, cut bias strips 1¼" wide. With wrong sides together, sew the fabric strips along the length ¼" from the folded edge and trim the seam allowance.

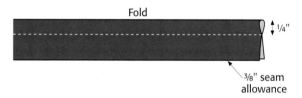

Fold

¼"

⅜" seam allowance

Insert the bias bar and position the seam at the center back; press.

Bias bar

A light spray of starch helps to hold the seam in place and keep the stem smooth and flat. Pin or baste the stems in place.

For fusible appliqué: Iron fusible web to the wrong side of the green print fat quarter. Do not peel off the backing paper. Square up the bottom edge of the fabric and place the 45° line of your ruler along the bottom edge, with the angled edge of the ruler passing through the corner of the fabric. Cut along the angled edge of the ruler. Slide your ruler along the fabric to cut ¼"-wide strips parallel to this line. Remove the paper backing to iron the stems in place.

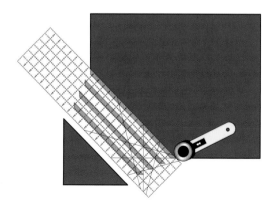

Appliqué the stems in place, ensuring that the ends of four of the shorter stems are positioned under the longer stems. Four other short stems flow over the top of the longer stems. With these, appliqué the base of the stems first and leave the ends free. When the long stems have all been appliquéd in place, return to the short stems, position them curving over the long stems, and appliqué them in place.

3. *To make the vase:* From a scrap of brown print, cut one vase from pattern A and appliqué in place.

4. *To make the leaves:* From the scraps of green prints, cut 16 leaves from pattern B and 2 leaves from pattern C. Appliqué in place, covering the raw ends of any stems.

5. *To make the flowers and buds:* From the scraps of brown prints, cut six from patterns D, E, and F; two from patterns G and H; one from patterns I, J, K, and L; and four from pattern M. Appliqué each flower piece in the order marked on the pattern sheet. *If doing hand appliqué,* make sure that a seam allowance is not turned under where the edge of that piece is to be covered by another appliqué shape.

6. When the appliqué is completed, trim the panel to 40" x 17" (100 cm x 43 cm).

Borders

1. From one 1"-wide dark brown strip, cut two pieces 17" long. Sew these strips to the sides of the quilt top and press the seams toward the borders. Sew the three remaining dark brown strips together end to end. From this long strip, cut two pieces 41" long. Sew these strips to the top and bottom of the quilt top and press the seams toward the borders.

2. From one 1½"-wide medium brown strip, cut two pieces 18" long. Sew these strips to the sides of the quilt top and press the seams toward the borders. Sew the three remaining medium brown strips together end to end. From this long strip, cut two pieces 43" long. Sew these strips to the top and bottom of the quilt top and press the seams toward the borders.

Finishing

1. Layer the backing, batting, and quilt top, smoothing each layer from the center outward as you go. Baste the three layers together using your preferred method.

2. Hand or machine quilt as desired. Coral hand quilted around the appliqué shapes and then crosshatched the background at 1" intervals.

3. Remove the basting and trim the excess batting and backing fabric even with the edges of the quilt top. Join the four 2½"-wide binding strips end to end using angled seams; press the seams open. Attach the binding to the quilt, referring to "Finishing" on page 109 for details.

4. Label your quilt, including your name, the date, and any other relevant information.

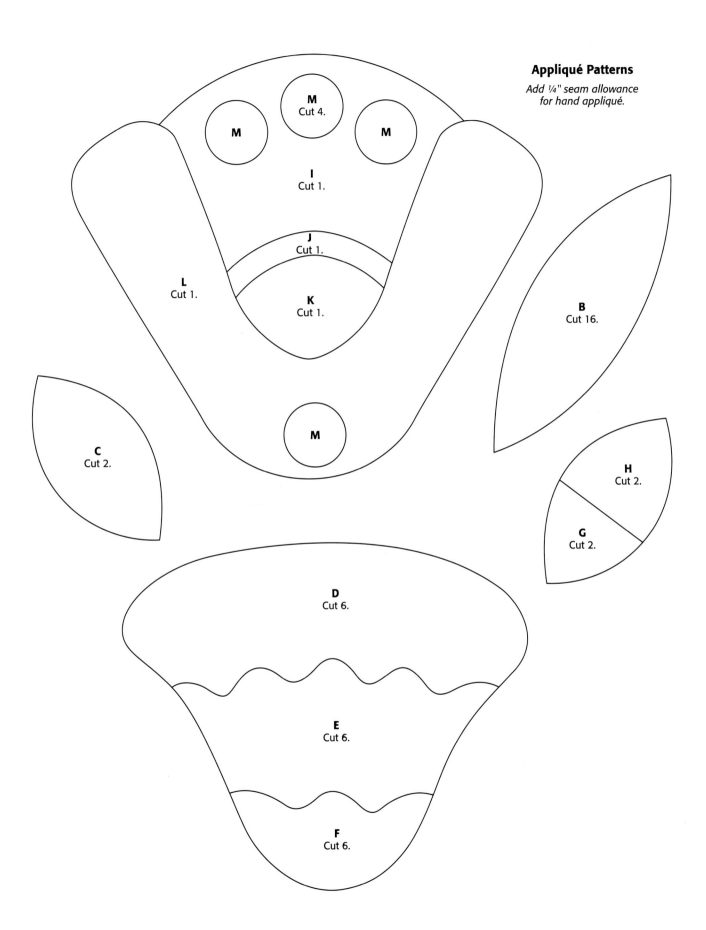

M
Cut 4.

M

M

I
Cut 1.

J
Cut 1.

L
Cut 1.

K
Cut 1.

B
Cut 16.

M

C
Cut 2.

H
Cut 2.

G
Cut 2.

D
Cut 6.

E
Cut 6.

F
Cut 6.

Appliqué Pattern

Add ¼" seam allowance
for hand appliqué.

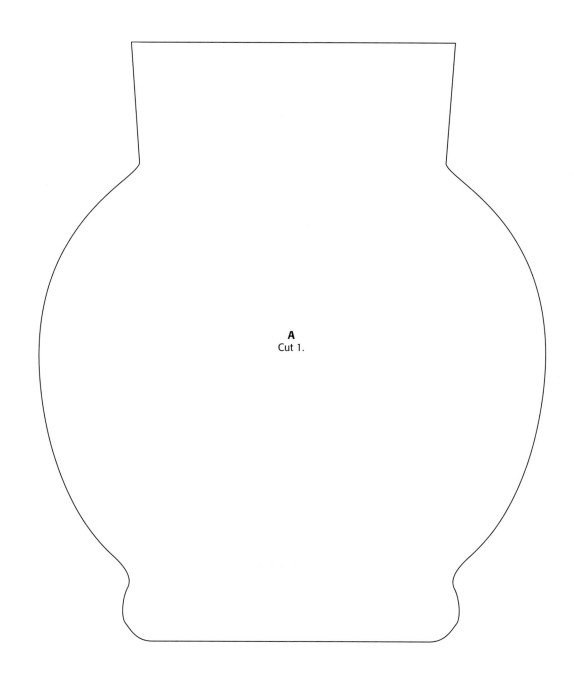

A
Cut 1.

Appliqué Placement Guide

Enlarge 400%.

Finished Quilt Size: 79½" x 91½" (202 cm x 232 cm) ▼ Finished Block Size: 6" x 6" (15 cm x 15 cm)

ANTIQUE PUSS IN THE CORNER

This exciting scrap quilt comes from the collection of Suzy Atkins. Made in the 1870s, the quilt demonstrates that blocks don't need to be complex to make a stunning impact. The block is a simple Nine Patch variation called Puss in the Corner. The maker of the quilt carefully sorted her lights and darks to make positive and negative blocks which, when set together, result in a visually complex design.

Although unusual now, quilts with borders on three sides were relatively common in the 19th century. Since the quilts would have been made for beds fixed or placed against walls, frugal quilters didn't deem it necessary to construct a border that would be hidden. The borders are also wider at what may have been the head of the bed. Suzy has provided instructions for the more regular four-sided borders. ❧

Materials

Amounts are based on 42"-wide (107 cm) fabric.

- ▼ 1½ yards (1.2 m) of beige floral print for first and third borders
- ▼ ¾ yard (55 cm) of striped fabric for second border
- ▼ 24 fat quarters of medium or dark-value prints for blocks
- ▼ 24 fat quarters of light-value prints for blocks
- ▼ 6¼ yards (5 m) of backing fabric
- ▼ ¾ yard (55 cm) of beige print for binding
- ▼ 86" x 98" (220 cm x 250 cm) piece of batting
- ▼ Reducing glass (optional)

Cutting

All cutting dimensions include ¼" seam allowances. Instructions are for cutting strips across the fabric width.

From *each* fat quarter, cut:

- ▼ 3 squares, 3½" x 3½"
- ▼ 12 squares, 2" x 2"
- ▼ 12 rectangles, 2" x 3½"

From the beige floral print, cut:

- ▼ 8 strips, 2" wide
- ▼ 9 strips, 3½" wide

From the striped fabric, cut:

- ▼ 9 strips, 2½" wide

From the beige print for binding, cut:

- ▼ 9 strips, 2½" wide

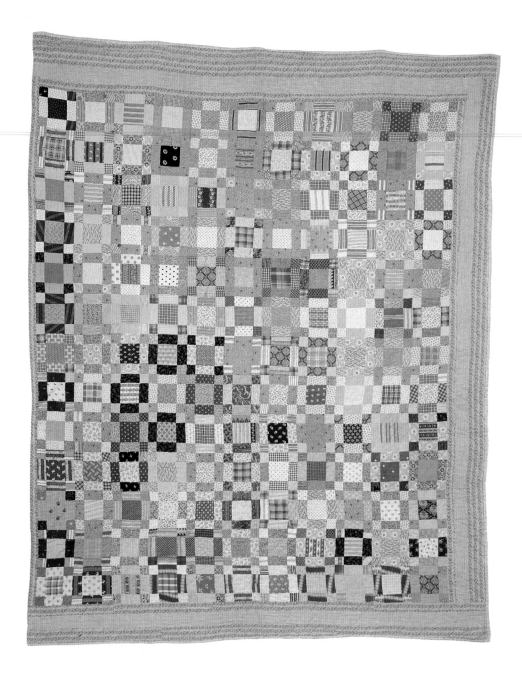

Fabric Selection

Most of the blocks in this quilt have three different fabrics. Some have only two and others have more. Also, many of the small squares are pieced from two or three smaller scraps. If you are after a truly authentic look, you may wish to do this, too. Even if you are using a range of reproduction fabrics, make sure that you vary the scale and the design of your fabrics. Too many floral prints will make a quilt look new. This quilt has many ginghams, shirting prints, and strips cut off-grain. Refer to the photograph of the quilt to see the variations of the light- and medium- or dark-value fabrics.

Block Assembly

Positive Blocks

1. Join a 2" medium or dark square to each end of two light rectangles; press the seams toward the squares.

2. Join a light rectangle to each side of a 3½" medium or dark square; press the seams toward the square.

3. Join the three rows together to complete the block and press the seams toward the center row.

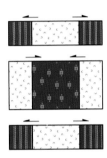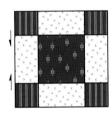

Make 72.

Negative Blocks

1. Join a 2" light square to each end of two medium or dark rectangles; press the seams toward the rectangles.

2. Join a medium or dark rectangle to each side of a 3½" light square; press the seams toward the rectangles.

3. Join the three rows together to complete the block and press the seams away from the center row.

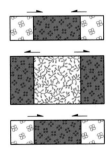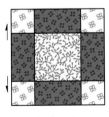

Make 71.

Quilt Assembly

1. Lay out the blocks in 13 rows of 11 blocks each. Odd-numbered rows will start on the left with a positive block, and even-numbered rows will start with a negative block. You can check your layout with a reducing glass to ensure that the colors and fabrics are evenly distributed throughout the quilt top.

2. Sew the blocks into horizontal rows, carefully matching the seams. Press the seams for each row in opposite directions so that the seams oppose when the rows are stitched together.

3. Sew the rows together, pinning them to match the block intersections. Press these seams in either direction.

Borders

1. Join the 2"-wide beige floral strips in pairs end to end.

2. Measure the length of the quilt top through the center; it should measure 78½". Cut two strips of this length from the long 2"-wide beige floral strips. Pin the strips to the sides of the quilt, easing to fit. Sew the borders to the quilt and press the seams toward the borders.

3. Measure the width of the quilt top through the center; it should measure 69½". Cut two strips of this length from the remaining long 2"-wide beige floral strips. Pin the strips to the ends of the quilt, easing to fit. Sew the borders to the quilt and press the seams toward the borders.

4. Cut one of the 2½"-wide striped strips into two 21" pieces. Join one of these pieces and two 42"-long strips end to end to make one long strip. Repeat with the other short strip and two more 42"-long strips.

5. Measure the length of the quilt top through the center; it should measure 81½". Cut two strips of this length from the long striped strips. Pin, sew, and press as in step 2.

6. Join the remaining four strips of striped fabric in pairs end to end.

7. Measure the width of the quilt top through the center; it should measure 73½". Cut two strips of this length from the remaining long striped fabric strips. Pin, sew, and press as in step 3.

8. Cut one of the 3½"-wide beige floral strips into two 21" pieces. Join one of these pieces and two 42"-long strips end to end to make

one long strip. Repeat with the other short strip and two more 42"-long strips.

9. Measure the length of the quilt top through the center; it should measure 85½". Cut two strips of this length from the long beige floral strips. Pin, sew, and press as in step 2.

10. Join the remaining four beige floral strips in pairs end to end.

11. Measure the width of the quilt top through the center; it should measure 79½". Cut two strips of this length from the remaining long beige floral strips. Pin, sew, and press as in step 3.

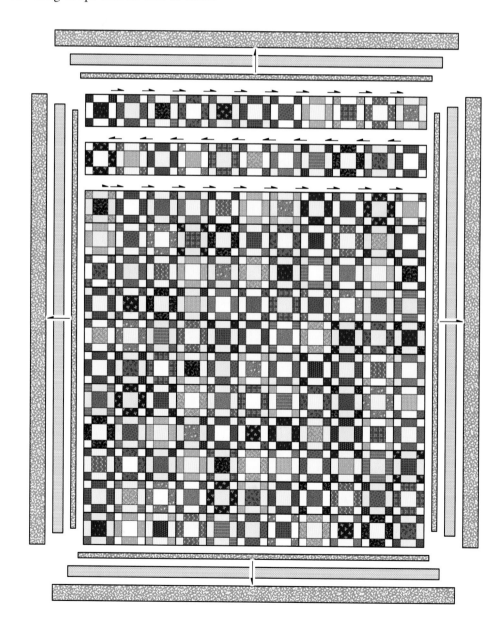

Finishing

1. From the backing fabric, cut two pieces 86" long and one piece 44" long and remove the selvages. Cut the 44"-long piece lengthwise into two 20" x 44" pieces. Sew these together end to end and trim this piece to 86". Sew the three 86" pieces together along their length to make a pieced back with two horizontal seams. Press the seams to one side.

2. Layer the backing, batting, and quilt top, smoothing each layer from the center outward as you go. Baste the three layers together using your preferred method.

3. Hand or machine quilt as desired. Suzy's antique quilt was hand quilted with 1" diagonal lines in one direction across all the blocks and in the opposite direction in the borders.

4. Remove the basting and trim the excess batting and backing fabric even with the edges of the quilt top. Join the nine 2½"-wide binding strips end to end using angled seams; press the seams open. Attach the binding to the quilt, referring to "Finishing" on page 109 for more details.

5. Label your quilt, including your name, the date, and any other relevant information.

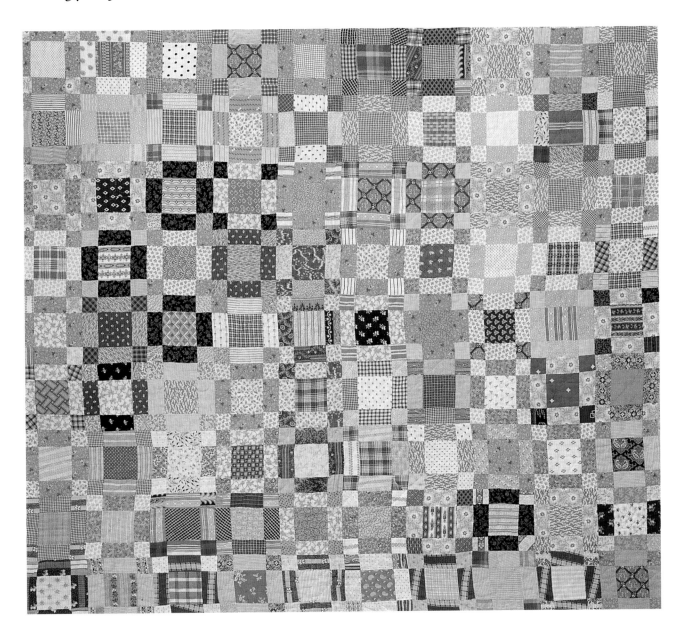

Finished Quilt Size: 85½" x 95½" (217 cm x 242 cm) ▼ Finished Block Size: 5" x 5" (13 cm x 13 cm)

ROSE DREAM

This beautiful quilt by Cindy Cudmore features a traditional pattern and would make a wonderful hand project. Attracted by the simple design and by her enjoyment of curved piecing, Cindy made this quilt using only two contrasting fabrics. Choose two favorite fabrics for your quilt, or make it from light and dark scraps in your collection. 🌹

Materials

Amounts are based on 42"-wide (107 cm) fabric.

▼ 8¼ yards (7.4 m) of pink tone-on-tone print for blocks, border, and binding

▼ 5½ yards (5 m) of white solid fabric for blocks

▼ 8 yards (7 m) of backing fabric

▼ 90" x 100" (225 x 250) piece of batting

▼ Template plastic

Cutting

All cutting dimensions include ¼" seam allowances. Instructions are for cutting strips across the fabric width except where noted.

From the pink tone-on-tone print, cut *lengthwise*:

▼ 2 strips, 8" x 80½"

▼ 2 strips, 8" x 70½"

From the remainder of the pink tone-on-tone print, cut:

▼ 25 strips, 4¼" wide; crosscut into 224 squares, 4¼" x 4¼"

▼ 11 strips, 1¾" wide; crosscut into 224 squares, 1¾" x 1¾"

▼ 10 binding strips, 2½" wide

▼ 112 of pattern A

From the white solid, cut:

▼ 4 squares, 8" x 8"

▼ 25 strips, 4¼" wide; crosscut into 224 squares, 4 ¼" x 4¼"

▼ 11 strips, 1¾" wide; crosscut into 224 squares, 1¾" x 1¾"

▼ 112 of pattern A

Template A

1. Trace pattern A on page 67 onto template plastic and cut it out. Be sure to mark the center of the curves with a line or a dot.

2. Lightly trace template A onto the wrong side of the fabrics, marking the center of the curves. Cut out each piece, adding a ¼" seam allowance.

Pink Block Assembly

For each pink block, you will need two pink 4¼" squares, one white pattern A piece, and two white 1¾" squares.

1. Trace pattern B on page 67 onto template plastic and cut it out. Be sure to mark the center of the curve with a line or a dot. Place the template on the wrong side of each 4¼"

square and lightly draw the seam-allowance line, marking the center of the curve. Cut away the curved corner piece, leaving ¼" seam allowance past the drawn line.

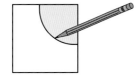

2. Sew a 1¾" white square to each end of 112 of the trimmed pink squares. Press toward the white squares.

3. Sew a white pattern A piece to the other 112 pink squares, matching the marks at the center of the curves. Press toward the white piece.

4. Sew a unit from step 2 and a unit from step 3 together, matching the marks at the center of the curves and the seam intersections. Press toward the white center.

Make 112.

White Block Assembly

For each white block, you will need two white 4¼" squares, one pink pattern A piece, and two pink 1¾" squares. Follow steps 1–4 of "Pink Block Assembly" to make these blocks and simply reverse the colors in each position.

Make 112.

Quilt Assembly

The quilt is constructed in 16 rows of 14 blocks each.

1. Referring to the assembly diagram, start row 1 with a pink block and start row 2 with a white block. Be sure that the placement of the A piece is the same for all the pink blocks and lies in the opposite direction to all the white blocks. Sew the blocks together and press the seams toward the pink blocks. Make 16 rows.

2. Sew the rows together, carefully butting the seam intersections.

Assembly Diagram

Border

1. Sew the two 80½"-long pink strips to the sides of the quilt top. Press the seams toward the borders.

2. Join an 8" white square to each end of the 70½"-long pink strips. Sew these borders to the top and bottom of the quilt top and press the seams toward the borders.

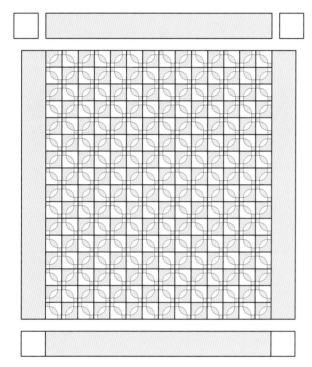

Finishing

1. Cut the backing fabric into three equal lengths, remove the selvages, and sew the three pieces together along their length to make a backing with two horizontal seams. Press the seams to one side. You may wish to trim the length to 100".

2. Layer the backing, batting, and quilt top, smoothing each layer from the center outward as you go. Baste the three layers together using your preferred method.

3. Hand or machine quilt as desired. The quilting design came from a photograph of an antique quilt in Jenny Manning's book *Australia's Quilts: A Directory of Patchwork Treasures.* This quilt was stitched in the ditch around the large square pieces and along the inner edge of the border. It was quilted in a diagonal grid across the quilt, through the center of each A piece and four-patch unit. Three lines were quilted in each large square, echoing the outer edge, and it was also quilted around the A pieces. The border was quilted with a large feathered cable.

4. Remove the basting and trim the excess batting and backing fabric even with the edges of the quilt top. Join the ten 2½"-wide binding strips end to end using angled seams; press the seams open. Attach the binding to the quilt, referring to "Finishing" on page 109 for more details.

5. Label your quilt, including your name, the date, and any other relevant information.

Piecing Patterns

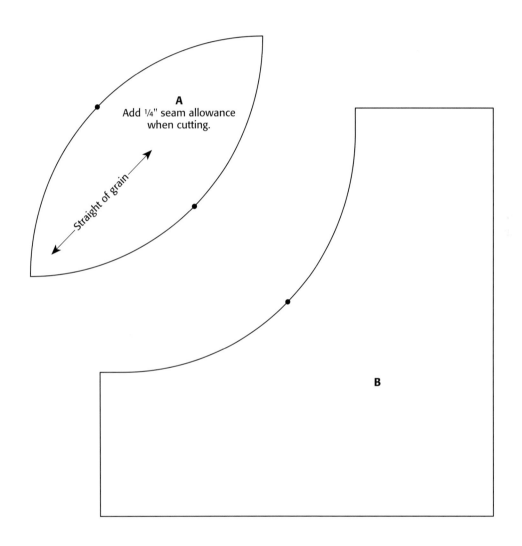

A
Add ¼" seam allowance when cutting.

Straight of grain

B

Finished Quilt Size: 40" x 40" (102 cm square) ▼ Finished Block Size: 8" x 8" (20 cm x 20 cm)

BLUE STAR GARDEN

This quilt by Yvonne Skodt, a combination of quick-piecing techniques and beautiful appliqué, is a pleasure to make. Its fresh blue stars and flowers are highlighted against a crisp white background. 🌼

Materials

Amounts are based on 42"-wide (107 cm) fabric.

▼ 1½ yards (1.3 m) of white muslin for borders and background

▼ 1¼ yards (1.1 m) of dark blue mottled print for star points, appliqué, and binding

▼ ¼ yard (20 cm) *each* of 6 coordinating blue prints

▼ ¼ yard (20 cm) of light blue marbled print for appliqué

▼ 1¼ yards (1.1 m) of backing fabric

▼ 45" x 45" (115 cm x 115 cm) piece of batting

▼ Dark blue embroidery thread

▼ 24 small blue buttons (optional)

▼ ⅛" (3 mm) bias pressing bar

Cutting

All cutting dimensions include ¼" seam allowances. Instructions are for cutting strips across the fabric width except where noted.

From *each* of 2 of the coordinating blue prints, cut:

▼ 2 strips, 1½" wide

From *each* of the remaining 4 coordinating blue prints, cut:

▼ 3 strips, 1½" wide

From the dark blue mottled print, cut:

▼ 7 strips, 2½" wide; crosscut into 104 squares 2½" x 2½"

▼ 5 binding strips, 2" wide

From the white muslin, cut *lengthwise*:

▼ 4 strips, 4¼" x 44"

▼ 9 strips, 2½" wide; crosscut into 60 rectangles, 2½" x 4½", and 36 squares, 2½" x 2½"

16-Patch Assembly

1. Sew the 16 blue 1½"-wide strips into four sets of four strips, varying the combination of fabrics. Press the seams of each set in one direction. To avoid distortion, press long seams by placing the pieced strips across the ironing board instead of down the length. Crosscut the strip sets into 1½"-wide segments.

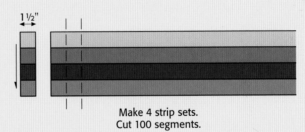

Make 4 strip sets.
Cut 100 segments.

2. Arrange four segments to form each 16-patch block. For easier piecing, make sure that each alternate segment has seams pressed in the opposite direction. Sew the segments together to make each block, matching the seam intersections. Press the seams in one direction.

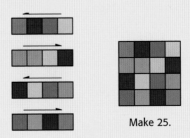

Make 25.

Flying Geese Assembly

1. On the wrong side of each of the 2½" dark blue squares, draw a diagonal line. Place a square on one end of a muslin rectangle with right sides together. Stitch along the line; trim the excess fabric, leaving a ¼" seam allowance; and press the dark blue fabric toward the corner.

2. Repeat this process with another dark blue square at the other end of the rectangle. Note that the diagonal slants in the opposite direction on either end of the rectangle.

Make 52.

Quilt Assembly

1. Using the assembly diagram and the photograph of the quilt as guides, arrange the 16-Patch blocks and the flying-geese units with the 36 muslin squares and the remaining eight muslin rectangles in 11 horizontal rows. Rearrange the 16-Patch blocks, if necessary, to achieve an even distribution of color throughout the quilt.

2. When you are satisfied with the layout, sew the pieces together in each row. Follow the pressing arrows exactly to have seams that will butt together perfectly. Sew the rows together to form the center of the quilt top. Be sure to match the seam intersections as you join the rows.

Assembly Diagram

Border

1. This border has mitered corners. Sew the 44"-long muslin strips to the sides of the quilt according to "Borders with Mitered Corners" on page 106.

2. Enlarge the appliqué border design on page 73 by 200% and trace the design lightly onto the right side of the borders with a pencil, tracing just inside the lines so they will be covered by the appliqué. Reverse the stem design and place it on the other side of the flower to trace the second side of each corner.

3. To make the stems, cut ¾"-wide bias strips from the remaining dark blue mottled print, referring to "Making Bias Tubes for Appliqué" on page 104. Fold the strips in half lengthwise with wrong sides together and stitch ¼" from the raw edge. Trim the seam to a scant ⅛". Insert the bias bar and press the stems flat, with the seams centered at the back of the strip. Position the stems along the traced lines, placing the short pieces first, then overlapping the ends with the long stems. Appliqué them in place as you go with thread that matches the stem fabric.

4. To make the flowers, buds, and leaves, trace the individual appliqué shapes onto the fabrics, adding a scant ¼" seam allowance. The leaves are cut from the dark blue mottled fabric, the petals and calyxes from the light blue marbled fabric, and the buds and flower centers from the leftover blue prints. Appliqué them in place, using your favorite method, with threads that match the appliqué shapes. Sew the petals and calyxes first, the flower centers and buds next, and the leaves last. Ensure that all the raw ends of the stems are completely covered by the appliqué shapes.

5. Yvonne embroidered tendrils that extend from each of the appliquéd stems. The dashed lines on the pattern indicate the embroidery sections of the design. Using one strand of dark blue embroidery thread, embroider the tendrils in stem stitch.

Finishing

1. Layer the backing, batting, and quilt top, smoothing each layer from the center outward as you go. Baste the three layers together using your preferred method.

2. Hand or machine quilt as desired. Yvonne quilted in the ditch of the piecing and appliqué, using dark blue thread around the 16 patches, and cream thread around the star points and appliqué designs. She then quilted more tendrils, extending from the floral border appliqué design with cream thread and using the dashed-line embroidery pattern.

3. Remove the basting and trim the batting and backing even with the edges of the quilt top. Join the five 2"-wide binding strips end to end using angled seams; press the seams open. Attach the binding to the quilt, referring to "Finishing" on page 109 for more details.

4. If desired, embellish the appliqué with a small blue button at the base of each flower bud.

5. Label your quilt, including your name, the date, and any other relevant information.

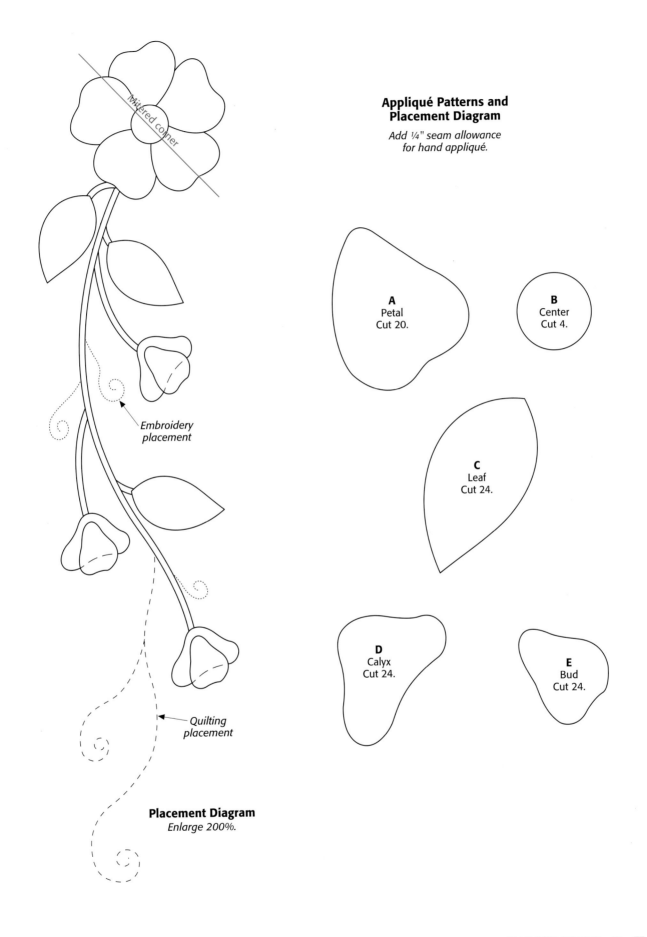

Mitered corner

Appliqué Patterns and Placement Diagram

*Add ¼" seam allowance
for hand appliqué.*

Embroidery
placement

Quilting
placement

A
Petal
Cut 20.

B
Center
Cut 4.

C
Leaf
Cut 24.

D
Calyx
Cut 24.

E
Bud
Cut 24.

Placement Diagram
Enlarge 200%.

Finished Quilt Size: 58" x 91" (145 cm x 231 cm) ▼ Finished Block Size: 8" x 10" (20 cm x 25 cm)

HEARTS AND BOWS

This lovely quilt by Judy Smith would make an adorable gift, and this one was made for Judy's little friend Andrea. The design lends itself to scrappy fabric choices, so it's a great way to use up some favorite scraps from your stash. This quilt is suitable for all skill levels and is a delight to make.

Materials

Amounts are based on 42"-wide (107 cm) fabric.

- ▼ 2½ yards (2.5 m) of background print for appliqué blocks and sashing
- ▼ 2 yards (1.9 m) of floral print for outer border and binding
- ▼ ½ yard (50 cm) of purple print for inner border
- ▼ 8 fat quarters of prints for hearts and corner-stones
- ▼ 24 scraps, 7" x 9" (18 cm x 23 cm), of assorted prints for strips around appliqué blocks
- ▼ 24 squares, 4½" x 4½" (12 cm x 12 cm), of assorted prints for bows
- ▼ 5½ yards (5 m) of backing fabric
- ▼ 62" x 95" (155 cm x 238 cm) piece of batting
- ▼ Fusible web (optional)
- ▼ Embroidery threads in colors to match appliqué fabrics

Cutting

All cutting dimensions include ¼" seam allowances. Instructions are for cutting strips across the fabric width.

From the 8 fat quarters, cut a total of:

- ▼ 35 squares, 3" x 3", for cornerstones
- ▼ 24 of heart pattern

From *each* of the 4½" squares, cut:

- ▼ 1 of bow and bow center patterns

From the background print, cut:

- ▼ 4 strips, 8½" wide; crosscut into 24 rectangles 6½" x 8½"
- ▼ 16 strips, 3" wide; crosscut into 30 strips, 3" x 10½", and 28 strips, 3" x 8½"

From *each* of the 7" x 9" scraps, cut:

- ▼ 4 strips, 1½" x 8½"

From the purple print, cut:

- ▼ 7 strips, 1½" wide

From the floral print, cut:

- ▼ 7 strips, 6" wide
- ▼ 8 binding strips, 2¼" wide

Heart Block Assembly

1. Using the appliqué method of your choice, trace and cut the heart and bow pieces from the patterns on page 79.

2. Position the hearts and bows onto the 6½" x 8½" background rectangles and pin or fuse them in place. Using embroidery thread to match each of the appliqué fabrics, blanket stitch around each shape.

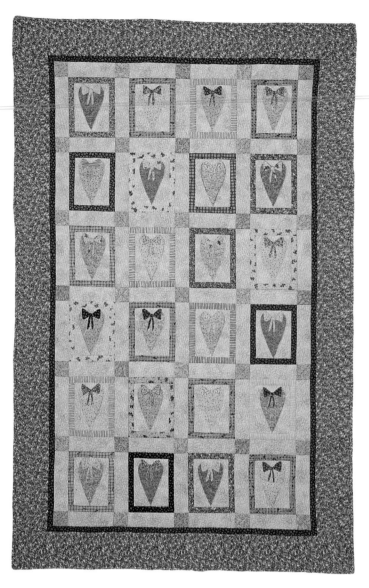

3. Sew a 1½" x 8½" strip to either side of the appliquéd heart block and press the seams toward the strips. Sew another strip to the top and bottom of each block and press the seams toward the strips.

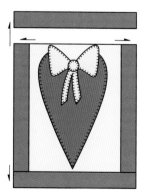

Make 24.

Quilt Assembly

1. Referring to the assembly diagram, lay out the blocks, the 10½" side sashing strips, the 8½" top and bottom sashing strips, and the 3" cornerstones. Sew the rows of cornerstones and sashing strips together and press the seams toward the sashing strips. Sew the rows of sashing strips and blocks together and press the seams toward the sashing strips.

2. Sew the rows together, carefully matching all seam intersections, and press the seams toward the cornerstone rows.

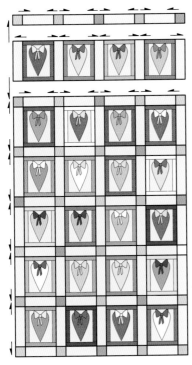

Assembly Diagram

Borders

1. Join four of the 1½"-wide purple strips in pairs, end to end. Measure the length of the quilt top through the center; it should measure 78". Cut two strips of this length from the long purple strips. Pin the strips to the sides of the quilt, easing to fit. Sew the borders to the quilt and press the seams toward the borders.

2. Cut one of the remaining 1½"-wide purple strips into two 21"-long pieces. Join one of these pieces and one 42"-long strip end to end to make one long strip. Repeat with the other short strip and one more 42"-long strip. Measure the width of the quilt top through the center; it should measure 47". Cut two strips of this length from these long purple strips. Pin the strips to the top and bottom of the quilt, easing to fit. Sew the borders to the quilt and press the seams toward the borders.

3. Join four of the 6"-wide floral strips in pairs end to end. Measure the length of the quilt top through the center; it should now measure 80". Cut two strips of this length from the long floral strips. Pin the strips to the sides of the quilt, easing to fit. Sew the borders to the quilt and press the seams toward the borders.

4. Cut one of the remaining 6"-wide floral strips into two 21"-long pieces. Join one of these pieces and one 42"-long strip end to end to make one long strip. Repeat with the other short strip and one more 42"-long strip. Measure the width of the quilt top through the center; it should measure 58". Cut two strips of this length from these long floral strips. Pin the strips to the top and bottom of the quilt, easing to fit. Sew the borders to the quilt and press the seams toward the borders.

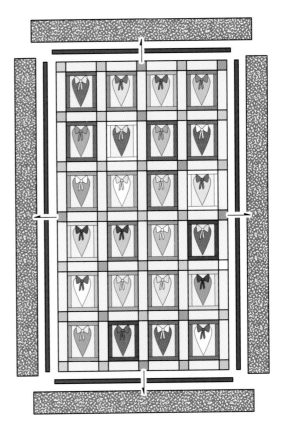

Finishing

1. Cut the backing fabric into two equal lengths, remove the selvages, and sew the two pieces together along the length to make a backing with a vertical seam. Press the seam to one side.

2. Layer the backing, batting, and quilt top, smoothing each layer from the center outward as you go. Baste the three layers together using your preferred method.

3. Hand or machine quilt as desired. This quilt was professionally machine quilted in a stipple pattern in the background of the blocks and in the sashing. Each block and border strip was quilted in the ditch, and the outer border was quilted in a large loop design.

4. Remove the basting and trim the batting and backing even with the edges of the quilt top. Join the eight 2¼"-wide binding strips end to end using angled seams; press the seams open. Attach the binding to the quilt, referring to "Finishing" on page 109 for more details.

5. Label your quilt, including your name, the date, and any other relevant information.

Just for fun! Sew a coloful button to the center of each bow.

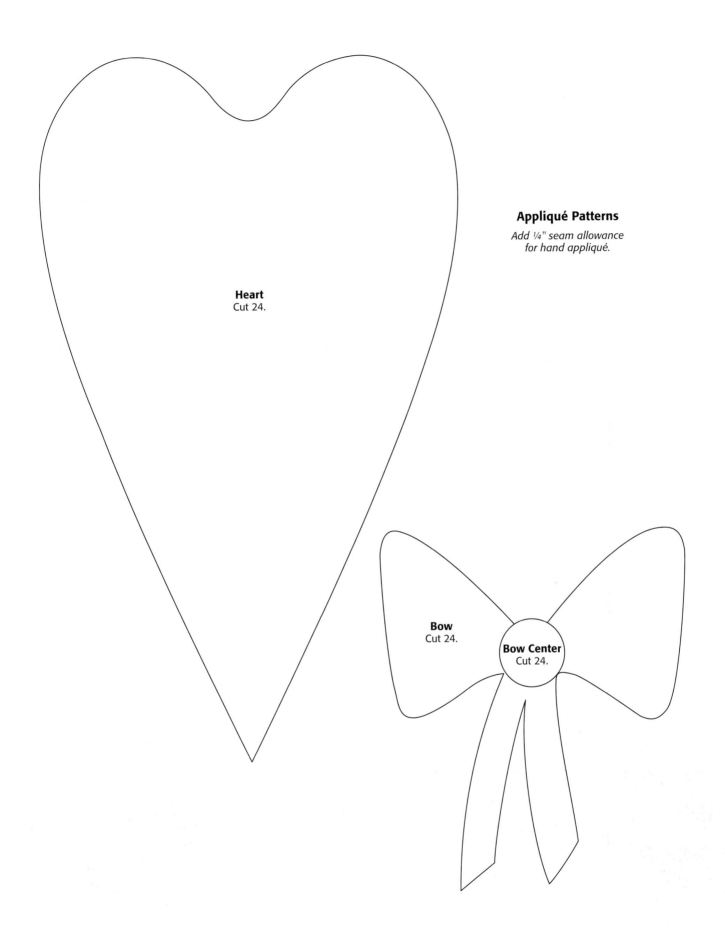

Heart
Cut 24.

Appliqué Patterns

*Add ¼" seam allowance
for hand appliqué.*

Bow
Cut 24.

Bow Center
Cut 24.

Finished Quilt Size: 85½" x 97½" (217 cm x 248 cm) ▼ Finished Block Size: 20" x 20" (51 cm x 51 cm)

 # Spring Garden

Well known for her timeless quilt designs, Karen Cunningham says her projects are often influenced by antique quilts and reproduction fabrics. Combining her love of piecing and appliqué with a beautiful palette of fabrics, Karen has made a wonderful quilt—the perfect project for spring. This quilt was machine quilted by Kay Brown, New South Wales, Australia. 🌸

Materials

Amounts are based on 42"-wide (107 cm) fabric.

- ▼ 3 yards (2.5 m) of floral-stripe fabric for outer border
- ▼ 2¼ yards (2 m) of green solid fabric for center strip and inner border
- ▼ 2 yards (1.6 m) of light green tone-on-tone print for background of Flying Geese
- ▼ 1¾ yards (1.6 m) of assorted red prints for Flying Geese
- ▼ 1½ yards (1.4 m) of large-scale floral print to set appliqué blocks square
- ▼ 1 yard (90 cm) of green print to set appliqué blocks on point
- ▼ ¾ yard (70 cm) of muslin for block backgrounds
- ▼ Assorted scrap fabrics for appliqué, Hourglass, and Four Patch blocks
- ▼ 7½ yards (7 m) of backing fabric
- ▼ ⅞ yard (80 cm) of red-and-white polka-dot fabric for binding
- ▼ 90" x 102" (231 cm x 264 cm) piece of batting
- ▼ Freezer paper

Cutting

All cutting dimensions include ¼" seam allowances. Instructions are for cutting strips across the fabric width except where noted.

From the muslin, cut:

- ▼ 2 strips, 11" wide; crosscut into 6 squares, 11" x 11"

From the green print, cut:

- ▼ 3 strips, 8½" wide; crosscut into 12 squares, 8½" x 8½"; cut squares once diagonally to yield 24 triangles

From the large-scale floral print, cut:

- ▼ 4 strips, 12" wide; crosscut into 12 squares, 12" x 12"; cut squares once diagonally to yield 24 triangles

From the light green tone-on-tone print, cut:

- ▼ 25 strips, 2½" wide; crosscut into 400 squares, 2½" x 2½"

From the assorted red prints, cut:

- ▼ 200 rectangles, 2½" x 4½"

From the assorted scrap fabrics, cut:

- ▼ 8 strips, 2½" x 12"
- ▼ 8 squares, 5¼" x 5¼"; cut squares twice diagonally to yield 32 quarter-square triangles

From the green solid fabric, cut *lengthwise*:

- ▼ 1 strip, 8½" x 76½"
- ▼ 2 strips, 2½" x 76½"
- ▼ 2 strips, 2½" x 68½"

From the floral-stripe fabric, cut *lengthwise*:

- ▼ 2 strips, 9" x 100"
- ▼ 2 strips, 9" x 88"

From the red-and-white polka-dot, cut:

- ▼ 10 strips, 2½" wide

Appliqué Block Assembly

1. Enlarge the appliqué block designs on pages 86–91 by 133% and lightly trace the designs onto the 11" muslin squares.

2. Select fabrics for each appliqué piece, using the photograph of the quilt as a guide.

3. Using the appliqué method of your choice, trace and cut all the appliqué pieces from the patterns on pages 86–91. The thin lines on the block designs represent ¼"-wide stems. Cut the stems on the bias grain of the fabric.

4. Beginning with the stems, pin the appliqué pieces to the background and appliqué them all in place. Use thread to match each appliqué piece. Begin with the center of the design and work outward. Appliqué flowers with multiple pieces in the order marked on the placement diagram. When completed, press the blocks from the wrong side and trim the blocks to 10½", making sure to keep the block design centered.

5. Sew the long side of two green print triangles to the opposite sides of each appliqué block and press the seams toward the green triangles. Sew two more triangles to the remaining sides in the same manner. Trim the blocks to 14¾", ensuring there is a ¼" seam allowance at each point in the block.

6. Sew the long side of four floral triangles to the blocks in the same manner as above and press the seams toward the floral triangles. Trim the blocks to 20½", ensuring there is a ¼" seam allowance at each point in the block.

Flying-Geese Units

1. Draw a diagonal line on the wrong side of each of the 2½" light green squares. Place a square on one end of a 2½" x 4½" red rectangle with right sides together. Stitch along the line; trim the excess fabric, leaving a ¼" seam allowance; and press the green fabric toward the corner.

2. Repeat this process with another square at the other end of the rectangle. Note that the diagonal slants in the opposite direction on either end of the rectangle.

Make 200.

3. Sew the completed flying-geese units together along the long edges to form 20 rows of 10 Flying Geese strips. When sewing the flying-geese units together, make sure you stitch above the crossed lines of the stitching on the wrong side of each unit to ensure you do not lose the points.

Four Patch Blocks

1. Sew the eight 2½" x 12" strips from the assorted scraps together in pairs along their length and press the seam to one side. Crosscut the strips into 16 segments, 2½" wide.

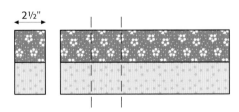

2. Sew the segments together to make the blocks, matching the seam intersections, and press. Vary the combination of fabrics for a scrappier look.

Make 8.

Hourglass Blocks

1. Sew the 32 quarter-square triangles together in pairs along the short edge as shown. Press the seams to one side.

2. Sew these 16 units together in pairs along the long edge to form eight squares. Once again, vary the combination of fabrics.

Make 16. Make 8.

Center Appliqué Strip

1. From the patterns on page 85, trace seven of center B onto the dull side of the freezer paper and carefully cut them out on the drawn line. Trace 42 of petal A onto the dull side of the freezer paper and carefully cut them out.

2. With the shiny side down, press the freezer-paper shapes to the wrong side of the selected fabrics and cut them out, adding a ¼" seam allowance all the way around. Turn over the seam allowances and baste them in place.

3. Whipstitch the six flower petals to each hexagon and then whipstitch the side seams of the flower petals. If the stitches show on the front of two pieces that are whipstitched together, it usually means that you are taking up too much of the fold of the fabric in the stitching.

4. Carefully press each flower and then remove the freezer paper, trimming any excess fabric from the seams to ensure a nice sharp point on the tip of each flower petal.

5. Fold the green solid 8½"-wide center strip across the width; fold it again, and fold it one more time so you have eight layers. Gently press both ends with the folds. Open it up and center a flower over each of the fold lines on the right side of the fabric. Appliqué the flowers to the green strip.

Quilt Assembly

1. Using the assembly diagram as a guide, lay out the completed appliqué blocks, appliqué strip, Flying Geese strips, and Hourglass and Four Patch blocks.

2. Sew a Flying Geese strip to either side of the appliqué blocks and press the seams toward the block. Sew the Hourglass blocks and the Four Patch blocks to the ends of the remaining Flying Geese strips; sew these to the appliqué blocks to form two vertical rows of three blocks each.

3. Sew the block rows to either side of the central appliqué strip, ensuring that each block is aligned vertically, and press the seams toward the appliqué strip.

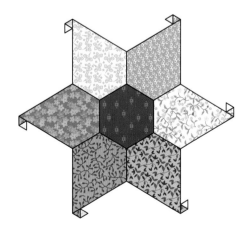

Assembly Diagram

Borders

1. Measure the length of the quilt top through the center; it should measure 76½". Sew the 76½"-long green solid border strips to the sides of the quilt top. Press toward the borders. Measure the width of the quilt top through the center; it should measure 68½". Sew the 68½"-long green solid border strips to the top and bottom of the quilt top. Press toward the borders.

2. The floral-stripe border has mitered corners. Add the 100"-long strips to the sides of the quilt and the 88"-long strips to the top and bottom of the quilt according to "Borders with Mitered Corners" on page 106.

Finishing

1. Cut the backing fabric into three equal lengths and remove the selvages. Sew the three pieces together to make a backing with two horizontal seams; press the seams to one side. You may wish to trim the back to 102" long.

2. Layer the backing, batting, and quilt top, smoothing each layer from the center outward as you go. Baste the three layers together using your preferred method.

3. Hand or machine quilt as desired. The featured quilt was machine quilted in ecru-colored thread. The appliqué blocks and the central appliqué strip were crosshatched with a ½" diagonal grid, and the motifs were quilted in the triangle sections of the block. The borders were quilted with different continuous-line designs.

4. Remove the basting and trim the excess batting and backing fabric even with the edges of the quilt top. Join the ten 2½"-wide binding strips end to end using angles seams; press the seams open. Attach the binding to the quilt, referring to "Finishing" on page 109 for more details.

5. Label your quilt, including your name, the date, and any other relevant information.

Appliqué Patterns

Add ¼" seam allowance for hand appliqué.

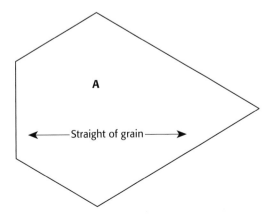

A

←— Straight of grain —→

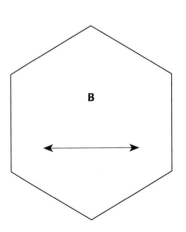

B

Appliqué Patterns and Placement Diagram

Enlarge 133%.

Add ¼" seam allowance for hand appliqué.

Center

Appliqué Patterns and Placement Diagram

Enlarge 133%.

Add ¼" seam allowance for hand appliqué.

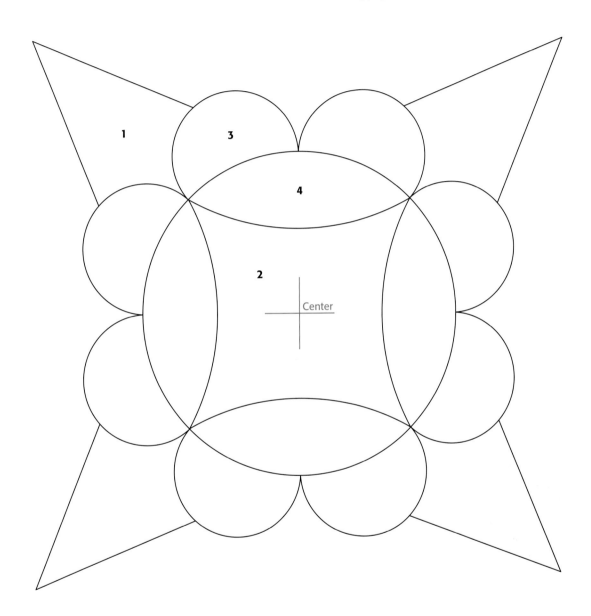

Appliqué Patterns and Placement Diagram

Enlarge 133%.
Add ¼" seam allowance for hand appliqué.

Center

Appliqué Patterns and Placement Diagram

Enlarge 133%.

Add ¼" seam allowance for hand appliqué.

Appliqué Patterns and Placement Diagram

Enlarge 133%.

Add ¼" seam allowance for hand appliqué.

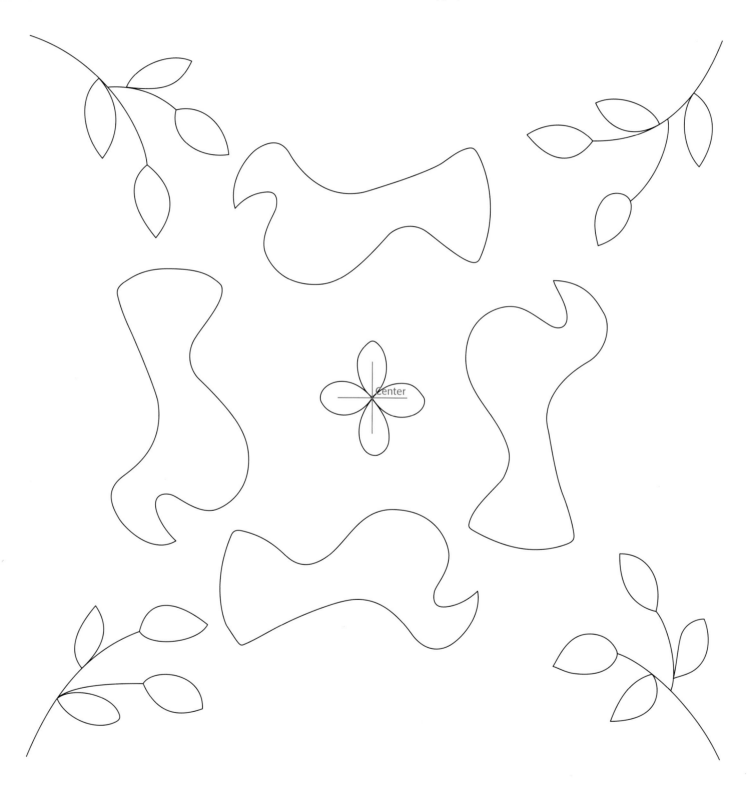

Center

Appliqué Patterns and Placement Diagram

Enlarge 133%.
Add ¼" seam allowance for hand appliqué.

Center

Finished Quilt Size: 73½" x 73½" (184 cm square) ▼ Finished Block Size: 12" x 12" (30 cm x 30 cm)

OLD-WORLD CHARM

This beautiful quilt made by Tracey Browning evokes the old-world feel of antique roses. For choosing fabrics, Tracey suggests selecting a rose print that is not too busy and then matching it with complementary fabrics. 🌹

Materials

Amounts are based on 42"-wide (107 cm) fabric.

▼ 2¼ yards (2 m) of rose print for blocks and third border

▼ 1½ yards (1.3 m) of light pink print for block background

▼ 1½ yards (1.3 m) of dark pink print for blocks and second border

▼ ¾ yard (70 cm) of light green print for large triangles in blocks

▼ ½ yard (40 cm) of medium pink print for sashing

▼ ½ yard (40 cm) of medium green print for small triangles in blocks

▼ ⅓ yard (30 cm) of dark green print for cornerstones and first border

▼ 4½ yards (4 m) of backing fabric

▼ 1 yard of medium pink print for binding

▼ 78" x 78" (200 cm x 200 cm) piece of batting

▼ Template plastic

Cutting

All cutting dimensions include ¼" seam allowances. Instructions are for cutting strips across the fabric width except where noted.

From the dark pink print, cut:

▼ 10 strips, 2½" wide; crosscut 4 strips into 64 squares, 2½" x 2½

From the light pink print, cut:

▼ 4 strips, 3½" wide; crosscut into 64 rectangles, 2½" x 3½"

▼ 4 strips, 4⅞" wide; crosscut into 32 squares, 4⅞" x 4⅞"; cut squares once diagonally to yield 64 triangles

▼ 3 strips, 5¼" wide; crosscut into 16 squares, 5¼" x 5¼"

From the light green print, cut:

▼ 4 strips, 5½" wide; crosscut into 32 rectangles, 4½" x 5½"

From the medium green print, cut:

▼ 3 strips, 5¼" wide; crosscut into 16 squares, 5¼" x 5¼"

From the rose print, cut *lengthwise*:

▼ 2 strips, 8½" x 60"

▼ 2 strips, 8½" x 75"

▼ 1 strip, 4½" wide; crosscut into 16 squares, 4½" x 4½"

From the medium pink print for sashing, cut:

▼ 1 strip, 12½" wide; crosscut into 24 strips, 1½" x 12½"

From the dark green print, cut:

▼ 6 strips, 1½" wide; crosscut 1 strip into 9 squares, 1½" x 1½", for cornerstones

Block Assembly

1. Sew a dark pink 2½" square to the short end of each of the 2½" x 3½" light pink rectangles. Press the seam allowance toward the rectangle.

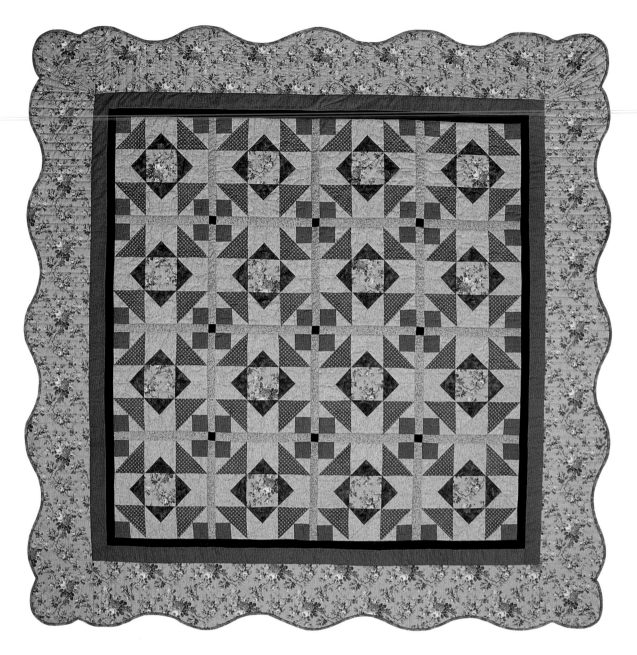

2. Sew pairs of square-rectangle units together as shown. Be sure to match the outside edges.

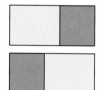 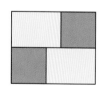

Make 32.

3. Clip the seam allowance just through the seam line in the space between the two squares. From the wrong side, press the seams

away from the squares, changing the direction of the seam at the center cut. There will be a small hole in the unit where you clipped, but you will eventually be cutting through this hole and it will not appear in your finished blocks.

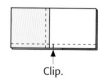 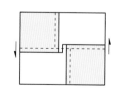

Clip.

4. Cut a 4½" square from the template plastic. Cut the template in half diagonally. You will use only one triangle.

Template plastic

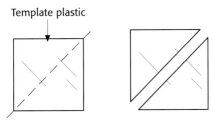

5. Place the triangle template on the wrong side of your pieced rectangles, with the corner of the template on the square. Draw the diagonal line as shown, ensuring it intersects with the point of the square on the seam line. Place the template on the opposite corner and mark a second sewing line.

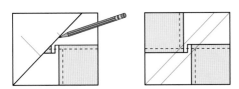

Pair the pieced rectangles and the light green 4½" x 5½" rectangles, right sides together, and sew on the marked lines. Cut the units apart, adding a ¼" seam allowance beyond the drawn lines, and press the seams toward the green triangles. You will make a total of 64 of these units.

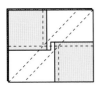

Make 64.

6. Draw two diagonal lines on the wrong side of the 5¼" light pink squares. Pair them, right sides together, with the 5¼" medium green squares. Sew ¼" from the drawn line, starting from the top left-hand corner and stitching to the solid line; pivot and stitch for ½" on the solid line, then pivot and stitch ¼" from the solid line down to the lower right-hand corner as shown. Rotate the squares a quarter turn and stitch along the other diagonal line in the same manner. Cut the four units apart on the solid lines and press toward the green triangle.

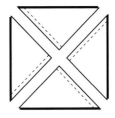
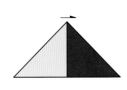

7. Pair these pieced triangles with the light pink triangles and stitch them together along the long side. Press the seams toward the larger triangle, and check that the unit measures 4½" square. You will make a total of 64 of these units.

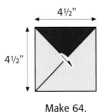

Make 64.

8. Using the block diagram as a guide, lay out the completed units and the 4½" rose squares in three rows of three. Stitch the units together to form rows, following the pressing arrows, and then stitch the rows together to form the block.

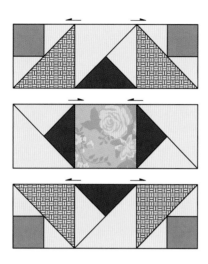

Make 16.

Quilt Assembly

1. Using the assembly diagram as a guide, lay out the pieced blocks with the light pink sashing strips and the dark green cornerstones. Sew the blocks, sashing strips, and cornerstones together into rows and press the seams toward the sashing strips.

2. Sew the rows together to make the quilt center. Press the seams toward the sashing strips.

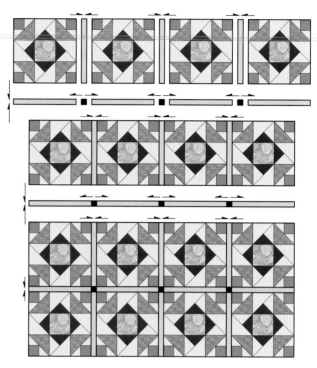

Assembly Diagram

Borders

1. For the first border, sew the five dark green strips together, end to end, to make one long strip. Measure the length of the quilt top through the center; it should measure 51½". Cut two strips of this length from the long strip. Sew the strips to the sides of the quilt top and press the seams toward the borders. Measure the width of the quilt top through the center; it should measure 53½". Cut two strips of this length from the remaining long strip and sew them to the top and bottom of the quilt top. Press the seams toward the border.

2. For the second border, sew the six 2¼"-wide medium pink strips together end to end to make one long strip. Measure the length of the quilt top through the center; it should measure 53½". Cut, sew, and press these side borders as in step 1. Measure the width of the quilt top through the center; it should measure 57½". Cut, sew, and press these top and bottom borders as in step 1.

3. For the third border, measure the length of the quilt top through the center; it should measure 57½". Trim the two 60"-long rose border strips to this length. Sew these to each side of the quilt top and press the seams toward the border. Measure the width of the quilt top through the center; it should measure 73½". Trim the two 75"-long rose border strips to this length. Sew these to the top and bottom of the quilt top and press the seams toward the border.

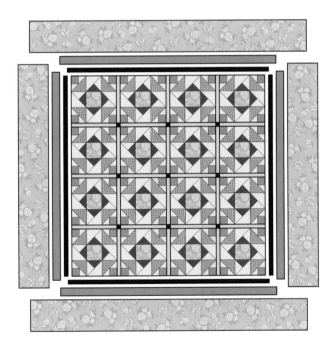

4. Using a large dinner plate or circle template, mark the curved edge of your quilt top, starting from the center of each side and working out toward the corners as shown. Tracey used a 12" plate for the edges and a smaller plate for the corners. Cut along the drawn line.

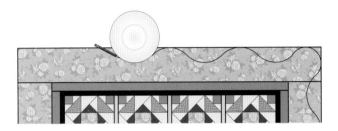

Finishing

1. Cut the backing fabric into two equal lengths, remove the selvages, and sew the two pieces together along the length to make a backing with a vertical seam. Press the seam to one side.

2. Layer the backing, batting, and quilt top, smoothing each layer from the center outward as you go. Baste the three layers together using your preferred method.

3. Hand or machine quilt as desired. This quilt was commercially quilted with a motif on each of the blocks and straight-line quilting in the third border.

4. Remove the basting and trim the excess batting and backing fabric even with the edges of the quilt top. From the medium pink print for binding, cut enough 2¼"-wide bias strips to equal a 320" length of joined strips, referring to "Cutting Bias Binding" on page 109. Attach the binding to the quilt, referring to "Attaching the Binding" on page 110 for more details.

5. Label your quilt, including your name, the date, and any other relevant information.

QUILTMAKING BASICS

Whether you're new to quiltmaking or you're simply ready to learn a new technique, you'll find this section filled with helpful information that can make putting your quilt together a pleasurable experience.

Fabrics and Supplies

Bias pressing bars: These narrow metal or nylon strips in assorted widths can be used to make stems for appliqué.

Fabrics: Select high-quality, 100%-cotton fabrics. They hold their shape well and are easy to handle. Regarding fabric measurements, the term *fat quarter* refers to 18" x 20" (45 x 50 cm) and *fat eighth* refers to 9" x 20" (25 x 50 cm) fabric.

Freezer paper: Freezer paper is plastic coated on one side and can be ironed onto fabric without damaging it. It sticks temporarily and can be removed and reused. It is often used to help make perfectly shaped appliqué pieces, and you can find it at your local grocery store.

Fusible web: This iron-on adhesive product makes any fabric fusible. Refer to the manufacturer's directions when applying fusible web to your fabrics.

Marking tools: Various tools are available to mark fabric when tracing around templates or marking quilting designs. Use a sharp No. 2 pencil or a fine-lead mechanical pencil on lighter-colored fabrics, and use a silver or chalk pencil on darker fabrics. Be sure to test your marking tool to make sure you can remove the marks easily.

Needles: A size 10/70 or 12/80 works well for machine piecing most cotton fabrics. A larger-size needle, such as a 14/90, works best for machine quilting. For hand appliqué, choose a needle that will glide easily through the edges of the appliqué pieces. Size 10 (fine) to size 12 (very fine) needles work well. For hand quilting, use Betweens, which are short, very sharp needles made specifically for this purpose.

Pins: Long, fine silk pins (with or without glass heads) slip easily through fabric, making them perfect for patchwork. Small ½"- to ¾"-long sequin pins work well for appliqué, although their shanks are thicker than silk pins.

Precut paper shapes: These are used for paper piecing, also known as English paper piecing. They are available at most quilt shops.

Rotary-cutting tools: You will need a rotary cutter, a cutting mat, and a clear acrylic ruler. Rotary-cutting rulers are available in a variety of sizes; some of the most frequently used sizes include 6" x 6", 6" x 24", 12" x 12", and 15" x 15".

Scissors: Use your best scissors only for cutting fabric. Use craft scissors to cut paper, cardboard, and template plastic. Sharp embroidery scissors or thread snips are handy for clipping threads.

Seam ripper: Use this tool to remove stitches from incorrectly sewn seams.

Sewing machine: To machine piece, you'll need a sewing machine that has a good straight stitch. You'll also need a walking foot or darning foot if you plan to machine quilt.

Template plastic: Use clear or frosted plastic (available at quilt shops) to make durable, accurate templates.

Thread: Use a good-quality, all-purpose cotton thread for piecing. For appliqué, use 100%-cotton thread or silk appliqué thread, which is widely available in most quilt shops.

Rotary Cutting

Instructions for quick-and-easy rotary cutting are provided wherever possible. All measurements include standard ¼"-wide seam allowances. If you are unfamiliar with rotary cutting, read the brief introduction below. For more detailed information, see *Shortcuts: A Concise Guide to Rotary Cutting* by Donna Lynn Thomas (Martingale & Company, 1999).

▼ Fold the fabric and match selvages, aligning the crosswise and lengthwise grains as much as possible. Place the folded edge closest to you on the cutting mat. Align a square ruler along the folded edge of the fabric. Place a long, straight ruler to the left of the square ruler, just covering the uneven raw edges of the left side of the fabric. Remove the square ruler and cut along the right edge of the long ruler,

rolling the rotary cutter away from you. Discard this strip. (Reverse this procedure if you are left-handed.)

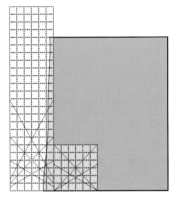

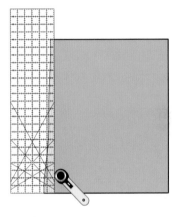

▼ To cut strips, align the newly cut edge of the fabric with the ruler markings at the required width. For example, to cut a 3"-wide strip, place the 3" ruler mark on the edge of the fabric.

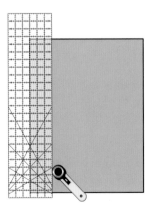

▼ To cut squares, cut strips in the required widths. Trim the selvage ends of the strips. Align the left edge of the strips with the correct ruler markings. The sides of each square should have the same measurement as the width of the strips. Cut the strips into squares. Continue cutting squares until you have the number needed.

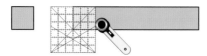

▼ To make a half-square triangle, begin by cutting a square 7/8" larger than the desired finished size of the short side of the triangle. Then cut the square once diagonally, corner to corner. Each square yields two half-square triangles. The short sides of each triangle are on the straight grain of the fabric.

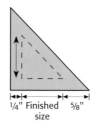

1/4" Finished 5/8"
size

1/4" + 5/8" = 7/8"

▼ To make a quarter-square triangle, begin by cutting a square 1 1/4" larger than the desired finished size of the long edge of the triangle. Then cut the square twice diagonally, corner to corner. Each square yields four quarter-square triangles. The long side of each triangle is on the straight grain of the fabric.

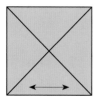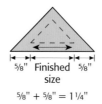

5/8" Finished 5/8"
size

5/8" + 5/8" = 1 1/4"

Machine Piecing

The most important thing to remember about machine piecing is that you need to maintain a consistent 1/4"-wide seam allowance. Otherwise, the quilt blocks will not be the desired finished size. If that happens, the size of everything else in the quilt is affected, including alternate blocks, sashings, and borders. Measurements for all components of each quilt are based on blocks that finish accurately to the desired size plus 1/4" on each edge for seam allowances.

Take the time to establish an exact 1/4"-wide seam guide on your machine. Some machines have a special quilting foot that measures exactly 1/4" from the center needle position to the edge of the foot. This feature allows you to use the edge of the presser foot to guide the fabric for a perfect 1/4"-wide seam allowance. If your machine doesn't have such a foot, create a seam guide by placing the edge of a piece of tape, moleskin, or a magnetic seam guide 1/4" away from the needle.

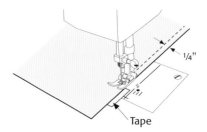

1/4"

Tape

Chain Piecing

Chain piecing is an efficient system that saves time and thread. It's especially useful when you're making many identical units.

1. Sew the first pair of pieces from cut edge to cut edge, using 12 to 15 stitches per inch. At the end of the seam, stop sewing but do not cut the thread.

2. Feed the next pair of pieces under the presser foot, as close as possible to the first. Continue feeding pieces through the machine without cutting the threads in between the pairs.

3. When all the pieces are sewn, remove the chain from the machine and clip the threads between the pairs of sewn pieces.

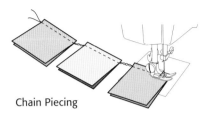

Chain Piecing

Easing

If two pieces being sewn together are slightly different in size (less than ⅛"), pin the places where the two pieces should match—and in between if necessary—to distribute the excess fabric evenly. Sew the seam with the larger piece on the bottom. The feed dogs will ease the two pieces together.

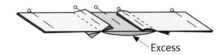

Excess

Pressing

The traditional rule in quiltmaking is to press seams to one side, toward the darker color wherever possible. First press the seams flat from the wrong side of the fabric; then press the seams in the desired direction from the right side. Press carefully to avoid distorting the shapes.

When joining two seamed units, plan ahead and press the seam allowances in opposite directions as shown. This reduces bulk and makes it easier to match the seam lines. The seam allowances will butt against each other where two seams meet, making it easier to sew units with perfectly matched seam intersections.

Opposing Seams

Appliqué Basics

General instructions are provided here for needle-turn, freezer-paper, and fusible appliqué. Even when a specific method of appliqué is mentioned in a project, you are always free to substitute your favorite method. Just be sure to adapt the pattern pieces and project instructions as necessary.

Making Templates

To begin, you will need to make templates of the appliqué patterns. Templates made from clear plastic are more durable and accurate than those made from cardboard. And, since you can see through the plastic, it is easy to trace the patterns accurately from the book page. It's preferable to use cardboard, however, when you need to gather fabric around the template and press to form a crease.

Place template plastic over each pattern piece and trace with a fine-line permanent marker. Do not add seam allowances. Cut out the templates on the drawn lines. You need only one template for each different motif or shape. Write the pattern name and grain-line arrow (if applicable) on the template.

Appliquéing by Hand

In traditional hand appliqué, the seam allowances are turned under before the appliqué is stitched to the background fabric. Two traditional methods for turning under the edges are needle-turn appliqué and freezer-paper appliqué. You can use either method to turn under the raw edges. Then use the traditional appliqué stitch to attach the shapes to your background fabric.

Needle-Turn Appliqué

1. Using a plastic template, trace the design onto the right side of the appliqué fabric. Use a No. 2 pencil to mark light fabrics and a white pencil to mark dark fabrics.

2. Cut out the fabric piece, adding a scant ¼"-wide seam allowance all around the marked shape.

3. Position the appliqué piece on the background fabric. Pin or baste in place.

4. Starting on a straight edge, use the tip of the needle to gently turn under the seam allowance, about ½" at a time. Hold the turned seam allowance firmly between the thumb and first finger of one hand as you stitch the appliqué to the background fabric with your other hand. Use a longer needle—a Sharp or milliner's needle—to help you control the seam allowance and turn it under neatly. Use the traditional appliqué stitch (see page 103) to sew your appliqué pieces to the background.

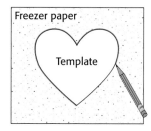

Pencil line

Freezer-Paper Appliqué

Freezer paper, which is coated on one side, is often used to help make perfectly shaped appliqués.

1. Trace around the template on the paper side (not the shiny side) of the freezer paper with a sharp pencil, or place the freezer paper, shiny side down, on top of the pattern and trace.

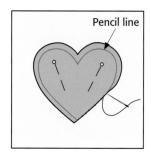

Freezer paper

Template

2. Cut out the traced design on the pencil line. Do not add seam allowances.

3. With the shiny side of the paper against the wrong side of your appliqué fabric, iron the freezer-paper cutout in place with a hot, dry iron.

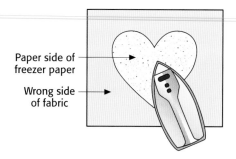

Paper side of freezer paper

Wrong side of fabric

4. Cut out the fabric shape, adding a ¼" seam allowance all around the outside edge of the freezer paper.

5. Turn and baste the seam allowance over the freezer-paper edges by hand, or use a fabric glue stick. Clip inside points and fold outside points.

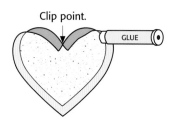

Clip point.

GLUE

6. Pin or baste the design to the background fabric or block. Appliqué the design, using the traditional appliqué stitch described on page 103.

7. Remove any basting stitches. Cut a small slit in the background fabric behind the appliqué and remove the freezer paper with tweezers.

If you used glue stick, soak the piece in warm water for a few minutes before removing the freezer paper.

Back of appliqué block

Traditional Appliqué Stitch

The traditional appliqué stitch or blind stitch is appropriate for sewing all appliqué shapes, including sharp points and curves.

1. Thread the needle with an approximately 18"-long single strand of thread in a color that closely matches the color of your appliqué. Knot the thread tail.

2. Hide the knot by slipping the needle into the seam allowance from the wrong side of the appliqué piece, bringing it out on the fold line.

3. Work from right to left if you are right-handed or from left to right if you are left-handed.

4. To make the first stitch, insert the needle into the background right next to where the needle came out of the appliqué fabric. Bring the needle up through the edge of the appliqué, about ⅛" from the first stitch.

5. As you bring the needle up, pierce the basted edge of the appliqué piece, catching only one or two threads of the edge.

6. Again, take a stitch into the background block right next to where the thread came up through the appliqué. Bring the needle up about ⅛" from the previous stitch, again catching the basted edge of the appliqué.

7. Give the thread a slight tug and continue stitching.

Note: The stitches in the appliqué illustration are enlarged to show placement. The stitches should not show in the completed work.

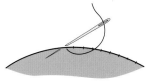

Appliqué Stitch

8. To end your stitching, pull the needle through to the wrong side. Behind the appliqué piece, take two small stitches, making knots by taking your needle through the loops. Check the right side to see if the thread shows through the background. If it does, take one more small stitch on the back side to direct the tail of the thread under the appliqué fabric.

Fusible Appliqué

Using fusible web is a fast and fun way to appliqué. If the appliqué pattern is directional, you need to make a reverse tracing of the pattern so the pattern will match the original design when fused in place. Otherwise, your finished project will be the reverse of the project shown in the book. You don't need to make reverse tracings for patterns that are symmetrical or for ones that are already printed in reverse. Refer to the manufacturer's directions when applying fusible web to your fabrics; each brand is a little different, and pressing it too long may result in fusible web that doesn't stick well.

1. Trace or draw the shape on the paper-backing side of the fusible web. Cut out the shape, leaving about a ¼" margin all around the outline.

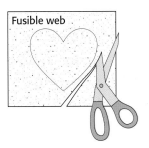

Fusible web

2. Fuse the shape to the wrong side of your fabric.

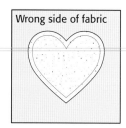

3. Cut out the shape exactly on the marked line.

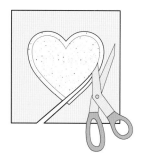

4. Remove the paper backing, position the shape on the background, and press it in place with your iron.

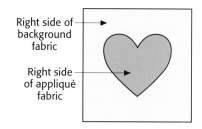

Making Bias Tubes for Appliqué

Bias tubes—often used for appliquéd stems and basket handles—are easy to make with the help of metal or nylon bias pressing bars. These handy notions come in sets of assorted widths.

1. Cut the fabric into bias strips the width specified in the quilt-project instructions, using a rotary cutter and a ruler.

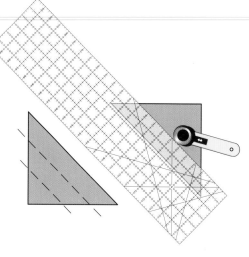

2. Fold each strip in half lengthwise, wrong sides together, and stitch from the folded edge, as specified in the quilt-project instructions.

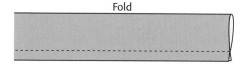

3. Insert a bias bar, roll the seam so it is centered along one flat edge of the bias bar, and press flat. Remove the bias bar.

Assembling the Quilt Top

From squaring up your blocks, to make them easier to sew together, to adding borders that aren't wavy, you'll find all you need to know about assembling your quilt top here.

Squaring Up Blocks

When your blocks are complete, take the time to square them up. Use a large, square ruler to measure your blocks and make sure they are the desired size plus an exact ¼" on each side for seam allowances. For example, if you are making 9" blocks, they should all measure 9½" before you sew them together. Trim the larger blocks to match the size of the smallest one. Be sure to trim all four sides; otherwise, your block will be lopsided.

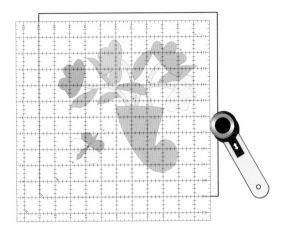

If your blocks are not the required finished size, adjust all the other components of the quilt, such as sashing and borders, accordingly.

Making Straight-Set Quilts

1. Arrange the blocks as shown in the assembly diagram included with the project instructions.

2. Sew the blocks together in horizontal rows, pressing the seams in opposite directions from one row to the next, unless directed otherwise in the project instructions.

3. Sew the rows together, making sure to match the seams between the blocks.

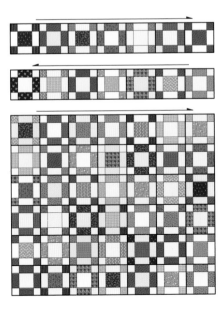

Adding Borders

For best results, do not cut border strips and sew them directly to the quilt without measuring first. The edges of a quilt often measure slightly longer than the distance through the quilt center, due to stretching during construction. Instead, measure the quilt top through the center in both directions to determine how long to cut the border strips. This step ensures that the finished quilt will be as straight and as "square" as possible, without wavy edges.

Many of the quilts in this book call for plain border strips. Some of these strips are cut along the crosswise grain and seamed where extra length is needed. Others are cut along the length of the fabric and do not need to be pieced.

Borders may have butted corners, corner squares, or mitered corners. Check the quilt pattern you are following to see which type of corner treatment you need.

Borders with Butted Corners

1. Measure the length of the quilt top through the center. Determine the midpoints of the border and quilt top by folding in half and creasing or pinning the centers. Then pin the borders to opposite sides of the quilt top, matching the center marks and ends and easing as necessary. Sew the border strips in place. Press the seams toward the borders.

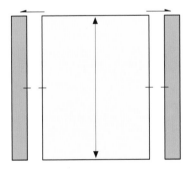

Measure center of
quilt, top to bottom.
Mark centers.

2. Measure the width of the quilt top through the center, including the side borders just added. Mark the centers of the quilt edges and the border strips. Pin the borders to the top and bottom edges of the quilt top, matching the center marks and ends and easing as necessary. Sew the border strips in place. Press the seams toward the border.

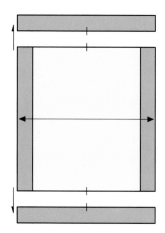

Measure center of quilt, side to side, including border strips. Mark centers.

Borders with Corner Squares

1. Measure the width and length of the quilt top through the center. Mark the center of the quilt edges and the border strips. Pin the side borders to opposite sides of the quilt top, matching the centers and ends and easing as necessary. Sew the side border strips to the quilt top; press the seam allowances toward the border.

2. Cut corner squares of the required size, which is the cut width of the border strips. Sew a corner square to each end of the remaining two border strips; press the seam allowances toward the border strips. Pin the border strips to the top and bottom edges of the quilt top. Match the centers, seams between the border strips and corner squares, and ends. Ease as necessary and stitch. Press the seam allowances toward the borders.

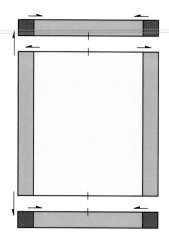

Borders with Mitered Corners

1. Estimate the finished outside dimensions of your quilt, including the borders. For example, if your quilt top measures 35½" x 50½" across the center and you want a 5"-wide border, your quilt top will then measure about 45½" x 60½" after the borders are attached. To give yourself some leeway, you may want to add approximately 4" more to those measurements. In this example, you would then cut two borders that measure 50" long and two borders that measure 65" long.

   Note: If your quilt has multiple borders, you can sew the individual border strips together first and treat the resulting unit as a single border. When mitering the corners, take care to match up the seam intersections of the multiple borders.

2. Fold the quilt in half and mark the centers of the quilt edges. Fold each border strip in half and mark the centers with pins.

3. Measure the length and width of the quilt top across the center. Note the measurements.

4. Place a pin at each end of the side border strips to mark the length of the quilt top. Repeat with the top and bottom borders.

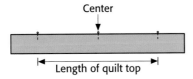

Center

Length of quilt top

5. Pin the border strips to the quilt top, matching the centers. Line up the pins at either end of the border strip with the edges of the quilt. Stitch, beginning and ending the stitching ¼" from the raw edges of the quilt top. Repeat with the remaining borders.

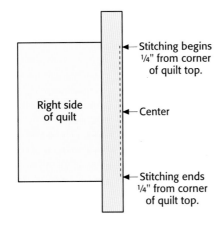

Stitching begins ¼" from corner of quilt top.

Right side of quilt

Center

Stitching ends ¼" from corner of quilt top.

6. Lay the first corner to be mitered on the ironing board, wrong side up. Fold the borders at a 45° angle at the corner, checking that the outer edges make a perfect right angle. Lightly press the folds.

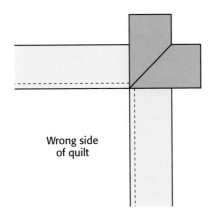

Wrong side of quilt

7. Fold the quilt with right sides together, lining up the adjacent edges of the border. If necessary, use a ruler and pencil to draw a line on the crease to make the stitching line more visible. Stitch on the pressed crease, sewing from the previous stitching line to the outside edges; backstitch where you start.

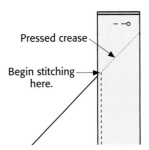

Pressed crease

Begin stitching here.

8. Press the seam open and check the right side of the quilt to make sure the miters are neat; then turn over the quilt and trim away the excess border strips, leaving a ¼"-wide seam allowance.

9. Repeat with the remaining corners.

Preparing to Quilt

If you'll be quilting your project by hand or on your home sewing machine, you'll want to follow the directions below for marking, layering, basting, and quilting. However, if you plan to have a professional machine quilter quilt your project, check with that person before preparing your finished quilt top in any way. Quilts do not need to be layered and basted for long-arm machine quilting, nor do they usually need to be marked.

Marking the Quilting Lines

Whether you mark quilting designs on the quilt top or not depends upon the type of quilting you will be doing. Marking is not necessary if you plan to quilt in the ditch (along the seam lines) or outline quilt a uniform distance from seam lines. For more complex quilting designs, however, mark the quilt top before the quilt is layered with batting and backing. Choose a marking tool that will be visible on your fabric and test it on fabric scraps to be sure the marks can be removed easily. See "Marking tools" on page 98 for options. Masking tape can be used to mark straight quilting lines. Tape only small sections at a time and remove the tape when you stop at the end of the day, or the sticky residue may be difficult to remove from the fabric.

Layering and Basting the Quilt

Once you complete the quilt top and mark it for quilting, assemble the quilt "sandwich," which consists of the backing, batting, and quilt top. The quilt backing and batting should be about 4" to 6" larger than the quilt top all the way around. Batting comes packaged in standard bed sizes, or it can be purchased by the yard.

For large quilts, you may need to sew two or three lengths of fabric together to make a backing. Trim away the selvages before piecing the lengths together. Press the seams to one side.

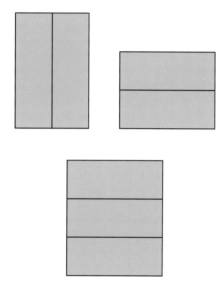

1. Spread the backing, wrong side up, on a flat, clean surface. Anchor it with pins or masking tape. Be careful not to stretch the backing out of shape.

2. Spread the batting over the backing, smoothing out any wrinkles.

3. Center the pressed quilt top, right side up, on top of the batting. Smooth out any wrinkles and make sure the quilt-top edges are parallel to the edges of the backing.

4. For hand quilting, baste with needle and thread, starting in the center and working diagonally to each corner. Then baste a grid of horizontal and vertical lines 6" to 8" apart. Finish by basting around the edges. For machine quilting, baste the layers with No. 2

rustproof safety pins. Place pins about 6" to 8" apart, away from the areas you intend to quilt.

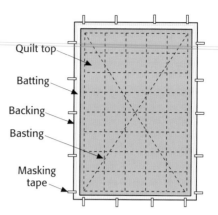

Quilt top
Batting
Backing
Basting
Masking tape

Quilting Techniques

Some of the projects in this book were hand quilted, others were machine quilted, and some were quilted on long-arm quilting machines. The choice is yours!

Hand Quilting

To quilt by hand, you will need short, sturdy needles (called Betweens), quilting thread, and a thimble to fit the middle finger of your sewing hand. Most quilters also use a frame or hoop to support their work. Use the smallest needle you can comfortably handle; the finer the needle, the smaller your stitches will be. The basics of hand quilting are explained below. For more information on hand quilting, refer to *Loving Stitches: A Guide to Fine Hand Quilting*, Revised Edition, by Jeana Kimball (Martingale & Company, 2003).

1. Thread your needle with a single strand of quilting thread about 18" long. Make a small knot and insert the needle in the top layer about 1" from the place where you want to start stitching. Pull the needle out at the point where quilting will begin and gently pull the thread until the knot pops through the fabric and into the batting.

2. Take small, evenly spaced stitches through all three quilt layers. Rock the needle up and down through all layers until you have three or four stitches on the needle. Place your

other hand underneath the quilt so you can feel the needle point with the tip of your finger when a stitch is taken.

3. To end a line of quilting, make a small knot close to the last stitch; then backstitch, running the thread a needle's length through the batting. Gently pull the thread until the knot pops into the batting; clip the thread at the quilt's surface.

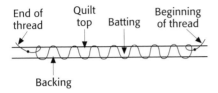

Machine Quilting

Machine quilting is suitable for all types of quilts, from wall hangings to crib quilts to full-size bed quilts. Marking the quilting design is only necessary if you need to follow a grid or a complex pattern. It is not necessary if you plan to quilt in the ditch, outline quilt a uniform distance from seam lines, or free-motion quilt in a random pattern.

For straight-line quilting, it is extremely helpful to have a walking foot to help feed the quilt layers through the machine without shifting or puckering. Some machines have a built-in walking foot; other machines require a separate attachment.

For free-motion quilting, you need a darning foot and the ability to drop or cover the feed dogs on your machine. With this type of quilting, you guide the fabric in the direction of the design rather than turning the fabric under the needle. Use free-motion quilting to outline quilt a fabric motif or to create stippling or other curved designs.

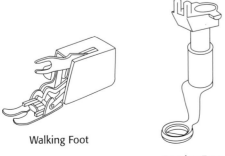

Walking Foot

Darning Foot

Long-Arm Machine Quilting

If you prefer to have your quilt quilted by a professional, ask at your local quilt shop for references about someone in your area who does this type of work. Generally, for long-arm quilting, you don't layer and baste the quilt prior to giving it to the quilter, nor do you have to mark the quilting designs. Check with your long-arm professional to be sure of specifications regarding batting and backing sizes before cutting or piecing yours.

Finishing

Bind your quilt, add a hanging sleeve if one is needed, label your quilt, and you're finished!

Cutting Straight-Grain Binding

For a double-fold binding, cut strips 2" to 2½" wide across the width of the fabric. (Some quilters prefer narrow binding, especially if a low-loft batting is used. If you're using a thicker batting, you may want to use 2½"-wide strips.) You will need enough strips to go around the perimeter of the quilt, plus 10" for seams and to turn the corners.

Cutting Bias Binding

1. Align the 45° mark of a square ruler along the selvage and place a long ruler's edge against it. Make the first cut.

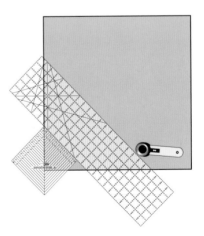

2. Measure the width of the strip from the cut edge of the fabric. Cut along the edge with the ruler. Continue cutting until you have the number of strips necessary to achieve the required length.

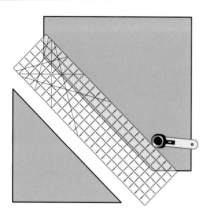

3. After making several cuts, carefully fold the fabric over itself so that the bias edges are even. Continue to cut the bias strips.

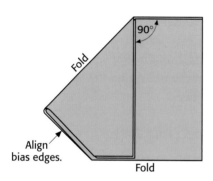

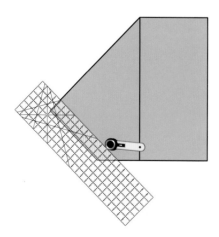

Attaching the Binding

1. Sew the binding strips together to make one long strip. Trim excess fabric and press the seams open to make one long piece of binding.

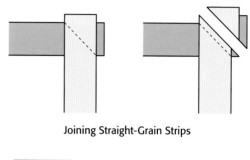

Joining Straight-Grain Strips

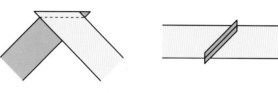

Joining Bias Strips

2. Fold the strip in half lengthwise, wrong sides together, and press.

3. Trim the batting and backing even with the quilt top. If you plan to add a hanging sleeve, do so now before attaching the binding (see page 112).

4. Starting near the middle of one side of the quilt, align the raw edges of the binding with the raw edges of the quilt top. Using a walking foot and a ¼"-wide seam allowance, begin

stitching the binding to the quilt, leaving a 6" tail unstitched. Stop stitching ¼" from the corner of the quilt.

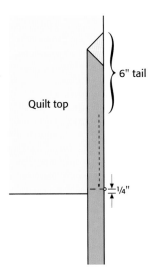

6" tail

Quilt top

¼"

5. Lift the needle out of the quilt, then turn the quilt so you will be stitching down the next side. Fold the binding up, away from the quilt, with raw edges aligned. Fold the binding back down onto itself, even with the edge of the quilt top. Begin stitching ¼" from the corner, backstitching to secure the stitches. Repeat the process on the remaining edges and corners of the quilt.

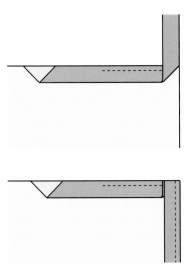

6. On the last side of the quilt, stop stitching about 7" from where you began. Overlap the ending binding tail with the starting tail. Trim the binding ends with a perpendicular cut so the overlap is exactly the same distance as the cut width of your binding strips. (If your binding strips are 2½" wide, the overlap should be 2½"; for 2"-wide binding, the overlap should be 2".)

2½" overlap

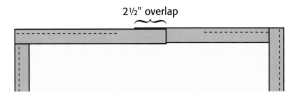

7. Open up the two ends of the folded binding. Place the tails right sides together so they join to form a right angle as shown. Pin the binding tails together, then mark a diagonal stitching line from corner to corner.

Pin ends together.
Draw diagonal line.

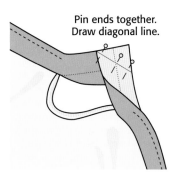

8. Stitch the binding tails together on the marked line. Trim the seam allowance to G"; press the seam open to reduce bulk. Refold the binding, align the edges with the raw edges of the quilt top, and finish sewing the binding in place.

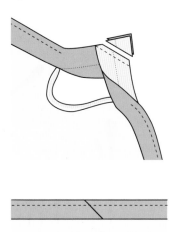

9. Fold the binding to the back of the quilt top to cover the machine stitching line. Hand stitch the binding in place, mitering the corners.

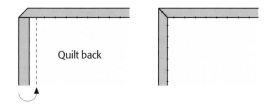

Quilt back

Adding a Hanging Sleeve

If you plan to display your finished quilt on the wall, be sure to add a hanging sleeve to hold the rod.

1. Using leftover fabric from the quilt backing, cut a strip 6" to 8" wide and 1" shorter than the width of your quilt. Fold the short ends under ½", then again ½" to make a hem. Stitch in place.

2. Fold the fabric strip in half lengthwise, wrong sides together, and baste the raw edges to the top of the quilt back. The top edge of the sleeve will be secured when the binding is sewn on the quilt.

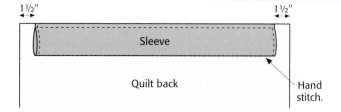

1½"   1½"
Sleeve
Quilt back   Hand stitch.

3. Finish the sleeve after the binding has been attached by blindstitching the bottom of the sleeve in place. Push the bottom edge of the sleeve up just a bit to provide a little give so the hanging rod does not put strain on the quilt.

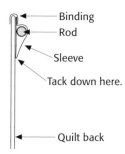

Binding
Rod
Sleeve
Tack down here.

Quilt back

Signing Your Quilt

Future generations will be interested to know more than just who made the quilt and when, so be sure to include the name of the quilt, your name, your hometown and state, the date, the name of the recipient if the quilt is a gift, and any other interesting or important background about the quilt. The information can be hand-written, typed, or embroidered.